Mammals of the Arabian Gulf

David L. Harrison

London
GEORGE ALLEN & UNWIN
Boston   Sydney

GEORGE ALLEN & UNWIN LTD
40 Museum Street, London WC1A 1LU

0189644X

British Library Cataloguing in Publication Data

Harrison, David L
 Mammals of the Arabian Gulf. – (The natural
 history of the Arabian Gulf).
 1. Mammals – Persian Gulf region – Identification
 I. Title   II. Series
 599.0953'6   QL729.P4   80–41340

 ISBN 0–04–59900–7

599.09536
HAR

Set in 11 on 12 point Times by Western Printing Services Ltd,
Avonmouth, Bristol
and printed in Great Britain by Biddles Ltd, Guildford, Surrey

This book is dedicated to the memory
of my brother Jeffery
whose enthusiasm and deep understanding
of Nature and of his fellow men was such an
inspiration to us all

Contents

8

Illustrations

PLATES

1a Long-eared hedgehog (*Hemiechinus auritus*)
 b Ethiopian hedgehog (*Paraechinus aethiopicus*)
 c Brandt's hedgehog (*Paraechinus hypomelas*)
 d Indian house shrew (*Suncus murinus*)

2a Naked-bellied tomb bat (*Taphozous nudiventris*)
 b Egyptian fruit bat (*Rousettus aegyptiacus*)

3a Honey badger (*Mellivora capensis*)
 b Indian grey mongoose (*Herpestes edwardsi ferrugineus*)

4a Arabian wolf (*Canis lupus arabs*)
 b Striped hyaena (*Hyaena hyaena*)

5a Asiatic jackal (*Canis aureus*)
 b Common red fox (*Vulpes vulpes*)

6a Arabian sand cat (*Felis margarita harrisoni*)
 b Fennec fox (*Fennecus zerda*)

7a Caracal lynx (*Caracal caracal*)
 b Wild cat (*Felis silvestris tristrami*)

8a Asiatic cheetah (*Acinonyx jubatus venaticus*)
 b Arabian leopard (*Panthera pardus nimr*)

9a Arabian tahr (*Hemitragus jayakari*)
 b Arabian oryx (*Oryx leucoryx*)

10a Arabian goitred gazelle (*Gazella subgutturosa marica*)
 b Arabian gazelle (*Gazella gazella arabica*)

11a Indian crested porcupine (*Hystrix indica*)
 b Cape hare (*Lepus capensis*)

12a Euphrates jerboa (*Allactaga euphratica*)
 b Arabian lesser jerboa (*Jaculus jaculus vocator*)

FIGURES

11

Preface

It gives me great pleasure to acknowledge here the invaluable help which I have received from my friends in the preparation of this book.

Special thanks are due to Maurice Wilson for his patient toil in preparation of the colour plates; also to Miss Vanda Salmon who has battled valiantly with the typescript. They are also due to Betty A. Lipscombe Vincett, whose superb book *Wild Flowers of central Saudi Arabia* has proved an invaluable aid. Perhaps my greatest debt lies with all those who have sent material or information to the Harrison Zoological Museum which has contributed so much to this study; space prevents me from naming them all but special mention must be made of Michael Baddeley; Michael P. Butler; William Büttiker; Michael D. Gallagher; Ralph Daly; John Gasperetti; Guy C. D. Harrison; Michael Jennings; Mark Legg; Robert E. Lewis; James P. Mandaville, Jr; Carl Seton Browne; and Patrick Granville White.

It would be most remiss not to record also my gratitude to all the local people who have assisted me in so many ways during my Arabian travels and without whose help this work would certainly have been impossible.

Harrison Zoological Museum   DAVID L. HARRISON
Bowerwood House
St Botolph's Road
Sevenoaks
Kent

Glossary of Terms

Aestivate
To become inactive and torpid during summer heat.

Antitragus
A lobe developed from the base of the outer margin of the ear-conch.

Arboreal
Of an animal, living habitually in trees.

Axilla
The cavity situated between the inner forelimb and the chest.

Brachyodont
Of teeth, having low crowns.

Calcaneum
A bone of the tarsus or ankle, forming the prominence of the heel in man and most mammals.

Canine
A single tooth, situated immediately behind the incisors in each jaw and generally tall and pointed in mammals.

Cannon bone
Bone between the fetlock and knee or hock of a hoofed mammal; the third metapodial of the horse and allied animals and the fused third and fourth metapodials of artiodactyls.

Carapace
The spiny protective covering of certain animals, eg. hedgehogs.

Carnassial
A specially modified cutting tooth in each jaw of a carnivore; pm^4 in the upper dentition, m_1 in the lower.

Cerebellum
The little or hind-brain of mammals, situated below and behind the cerebral hemispheres.

Cerebral
hemispheres
The large, paired, half-egg-shaped masses forming the bulk of the mammalian brain, of which the surfaces are convoluted.

Cingulum	A shelf round the margin of the crown of a tooth.
Cloaca	A common excretory opening for the urogenital and alimentary canals in primitive vertebrates.
Commensal	Of animals, such as rats and mice, living in close association with man, and subsisting at his expense, although capable of independent existence.
Crepuscular	Of an animal, active during the twilight hours.
Cribriform	Of a structure, with multiple sieve-like perforations.
Cuspidate	Of teeth, having the crowns composed of one or more conical cusps, or projections.
Dentine	The hard calcified substance that forms the main portion of a mammalian tooth; the layer beneath the enamel.
Diastema	A natural space in the toothrow, as in the rodents between the incisors and cheek-teeth.
Diurnal	Of an animal, active during the day.
Echolocation	The system of orientation by means of high frequency sound echoes, as employed by flying bats. The sound waves employed are inaudible to man and are called ultrasonic.
Enamel	The very hard substance forming the surface layer of the crown of most mammalian teeth, protecting the dentine.
Fibula	A long bone in the outer part of the lower leg, the more slender of the two bones usually connecting the knee to the ankle.
Foramen (pl. foramina)	An opening in a bone.
Fossorial	Of an animal, burrowing underground.
Frontal bone	Paired bones forming the front part of the vault of the skull.

Frugivorous	Of an animal, subsisting on a diet of fruit.
Gluteal	Of the buttocks or rump.
Gular	Associated with the throat.
Hypsodont	Of teeth, having high crowns, like the molars of most Bovidae.
Incisive foramina	A pair of openings in the bony palate, situated behind the incisor teeth.
Incisor	Front or cutting tooth, in the upper jaw situated in the premaxilla, the lower series in the front of the mandible.
Insectivorous	Of an animal, subsisting on a diet of insects.
Interfemoral membrane	Tail membrane of bats, extending from the back of the body and inner margins of the legs to enclose part or all of the tail, when this is present. Also known as the Uropatagium.
Lancet	Erect, subtriangular, posterior part of the noseleaf of a horseshoe bat of the genus *Rhinolophus,* the point of which forms the top of the noseleaf in these bats.
Mandible	Lower jaw bone of a mammal.
Mastoid	Part of the periotic bone of the skull, which is visible on the external aspect as a variably prominent mastoid process behind the ear opening.
Maxillary	The principal bone of the upper jaw and side of the face, containing the canine and cheekteeth. Also called maxilla.
Melanistic	Of animals, with excessive development of pigment melanin, producing a black colour variant.
Metacarpal	One of the long bones of the hand, extending from the carpal bones to the proximal phalanges of the fingers.

Molar	A back cheektooth of mammals, which has no milk tooth preceding it.
Nasals	The furthest forward bones (paired) on the roof of the skull, forming the roof of the nasal cavity.
Nasal inflations	Swellings of the bones of the nasal region.
Nocturnal	Of an animal, active at night.
Noseleaf	Specialised skin structure, developed round the nose.
Occiput	The lower back part of the skull, formed by the occipital bone.
Omnivorous	Having a variable diet.
Phalanx	A digital bone of a finger or toe (pl. phalanges).
Phallus	The male organ or penis.
Placental	Of higher mammals, the embryos of which are nourished by means of an after-birth or placenta.
Polymorphic	Of species, existing in several forms or types.
Premaxilla	The front bone of the upper jaw, containing the incisors, and contributing variably to the nose and palate.
Premolar	A mammalian cheektooth, having a milk precursor.
Psammophile	Of an animal, living in sandy places.
Radius	One of the two long bones of the forearm, on the same side as the thumb.
Ruminant	Of artiodactyls, having specialised stomachs with four compartments and which habitually regurgitate their food.
Secondary folioles	Additional leaflets developed at the edge of the horseshoe in the noseleaf of some leaf-nosed bats (*Hipposideridae*).
Sella	The inferior, saddle-like aspect of the

	median front projection of the noseleaf of a horseshoe bat (*Rhinolophus*) overhanging the top of the horseshoe.
Septum	An anatomical partition, separating structures.
Substrate	The soil or rock forming the habitat in which an animal lives.
Suprameatal triangle	A triangular area in the tympanic region of the skull of certain rodents, situated above the bony auditory meatus, and occupied by a part of the tympanic bulla.
Suture	Joint between two bones of the skull at their edges, often by an irregular junction and forming an immovable joint.
Tragus	A cutaneous and cartilaginous projection sometimes found at the opening of the external ear, especially developed in some bats.
Tympanic bulla	The usually rounded bony capsule surrounding the middle and internal ear of many mammals.
Tympanic membrane	Eardrum; a thin transparent sheet stretched across the passage leading into the ear and receiving the sound vibrations.
Vestigial	Of a structure only remnants of which persist.
Zygomatic arch	Arch of the cheekbones formed typically by the jugal bone in the central part, the maxilla in front and the squamosal behind.
Zygomatic plate	In the skull of rodents, a plate forming the outer wall of the infraorbital foramen and supporting the zygomatic arch below and in front.

Geographical Gazetteer

The following list consists of all those localities which are referred to in the text but which do not appear on the map of the Arabian Gulf (see endpapers); the localities marked on the map have not been duplicated on this list.

The map of the Arabian Gulf is reproduced in all volumes of the *Natural History of the Arabian Gulf* series.

Al Ain, UAE   24°15′N 55°45′E
Al 'Uwaynah, Saudi Arabia   26°46′N 48°24′E
Asimah, UAE   25°24′N 56°09′E
As Sarrah, Saudi Arabia   26°52′N 48°20′E app.
Bahrain Island, Arabian Gulf   c.a. 26°00′N 50°33′E
Batinah Coast, Oman c.a. 24°00′N 57°05′E app.
Dahana/the Dahana, Saudi Arabia   c.a. 26°00′N 47°00′E
Dammam, Saudi Arabia   26°25′N 50°06′E
Dibbah, UAE   25°39′N 56°15′E
Hasa/the Hasa, Saudi Arabia   c.a. 26°30′N 49°00′E
Howar Island, Bahrain   25°40′N 50°46′E
Jabrin, Saudi Arabia   23°20′N 48°56′E
Jebel Banban, Saudi Arabia   25°15′N 46°45′E app.
Jebel Faiyah, UAE   25°06′N 55°50′E
Jebel Hafit, UAE   24°55′N 45°00′E app.
Liwa, UAE   c.a. 23°30′N 53°30′E
Manasir Country, UAE   c.a. 23°20′N 52°45′E app.
Masafi, UAE   25°19′N 56°10′E
Nafud, Saudi Arabia   c.a. 28°30′N 41°00′E app.
Nejd Plateau, Saudi Arabia   c.a. 24°00′N 46°00′E app.
Qatar Peninsula   c.a. 25°00′N 51°15′E app.
Rubal-Khali, Saudi Arabia/South Yemen/Yemen/Oman
   c.a. 20°00′N 50°00′E app.
Safa, Saudi Arabia   27°48′N 46°50′E
Sayhat, Saudi Arabia   26°28′N 50°04′E
Sharjah, UAE   25°20′N 55°26′E
Summan, Saudi Arabia   c.a. 27°00′N 47°00′E
Tanb Island, Iran   26°15′N 55°17′E

Tawi Suwaihan, UAE   24°26′N 55°16′E app.
Tuwayq Escarpment/Tuwayq Mountains, Saudi Arabia
   24°35′N 46°18′E
Wadi Khumra, Saudi Arabia   c.a. 24°55′N 46°12′E app.

c.a.=centre at
app.=approximate location

Introduction

This guide to the mammals of the Arabian Gulf covers the countries forming the western shore of the Gulf, extending from Kuwait to Ras Musandam. The term shore has been used rather loosely here, however, and some species have been included which occur in eastern Saudi Arabia, although they have not as yet been found in the strictly coastal regions.

Although it is clearly impossible to write about mammals without using some technical terms, it should be emphasised that this is not intended as a technical work for specialists. It is designed for the interested layman who wishes to take an intelligent interest in the wild mammals he sees around him. For this reason detailed descriptions are reduced to a minimum, classification keys are as simple as possible and line drawings by the author are used to illustrate the essential features of the various species. Where more detailed information is necessary, the reader is referred to my monograph *The Mammals of Arabia* (Harrison 1964, 1968, 1972) which covers the fauna of the whole peninsula, and gives comprehensive information on each species.

The colour plates by Maurice Wilson, illustrating the present work, have been based on actual specimens in the Harrison Zoological Museum and have been designed to illustrate the distinctive features of the local species. This book therefore serves the purpose of a local field guide to the terrestrial wild mammals of the Arabian Gulf, but with the qualification that precise identification of many small mammals cannot be accomplished without reference to some features of the skull and teeth.

The Arabian shore of the Gulf, seen from the air, must surely appear one of the most dismal and inhospitable terrains on earth. The scattered centres of human settlement and the oil installations, which have so recently brought prosperity to this region, present a stark contrast to the flat, sandy wastes extending as far as the eye can see. These coastal regions form the north-eastern fringe of the great sand deserts of Rub al-Khali and Nafud, linked together by the sandy tract called Dahana, which together separate the Nejd Plateau of central Saudi Arabia from the coast. Only at the extreme southern end of this coastal area, in the Ras al-Khaimah peninsula, is the eye relieved by the rugged grandeur of the Oman mountains, reaching north to Ras Musandam and pointing like a gaunt serrated finger at the southern coast of Iran. Lush oases occur at scattered points in the desert interior, localities specially favoured by underground fresh water sources, such as Buraimi, Liwa and Hofuf: these sites are as important to animal life as they are to the human population of the region.

The mammalian life of the Arabian Gulf is surprisingly varied, in spite of the inhospitable nature of the terrain and climate. We are able to list in this book fifty species known to occur in the Gulf region. Quite a few others have been found in neighbouring parts of the peninsula and are given brief mention as, in the future, they may well be found to occur. Many of the species included in this book are especially fascinating for their profound and intricate adaptations for desert survival. Although space permits only the briefest consideration of such matters, it is hoped that this introduction will stimulate interest in some truly fascinating animals.

A book such as this will often be used to identify some small mammal kept in captivity as a pet or captured alive in the field. Although a definitive identification may not always be possible, it is hoped that the distinctive features of the various species illustrated here, together with the brief descriptions and keys provided, may at least enable a tentative conclusion to be reached. Dentition and measurements will often be helpful: by patient handling it is often possible to obtain useful information about the teeth of a living small mammal, while some external measurements are also readily taken from a living subject.

Order **INSECTIVORA** (Insectivores)

These are generally small, primitive placental mammals often recognisable externally by their long, narrow snouts. Eight living families occur throughout the world (except for Australia, Antarctica, Greenland and most of South America). In the Gulf only two families, the shrews (Soricidae), and the hedgehogs (Erinaceidae), are represented by one species of the former and three species of the latter.

The eyes are generally small; five clawed digits are present on each foot and, amongst other primitive features, many members of the order have a common cloacal opening for the genital and urinary systems. The teeth are primitive both in their large number and because of the sharply pointed cusps on the crowns of the cheekteeth, the dental formula* frequently being:

$$i\frac{3}{3} \; c \; \frac{1}{1} \; pm\frac{4}{4} \; m\frac{3}{3} \; or \; \frac{4}{4} = 44, \; 46 \; or \; 48$$

The braincase is relatively small and the brain itself has poorly developed cerebral hemispheres, lacking convolutions and not extending above the cerebellum. Most insectivores are terrestrial but some, like moles, are highly adapted for subterranean life; others, like water shrews and desmans, are aquatic. They are either nocturnal or diurnal and generally subsist on an insectivorous diet. The local species may be readily distinguished by the identification key overleaf.

* The dental formula is a simple way of expressing the number and type of teeth present in a mammal. i = incisors, c = canines, pm = premolars and m = molars. The figures above and below the lines represent the numbers of these teeth normally present in one upper and one lower jaw respectively. The sum of all these numbers multiplied by two gives the total number of teeth present (shown on the right).

Key to the Insectivora (Insectivores) of the Arabian Gulf

Body covered with short fur
Tail well developed, with long scattered hairs; ears small
Zygomatic arches (cheekbones) of skull absent (Fig. 2)
Large first incisor tooth with a second rear cusp (Fig. 1)
. . . Shrews (Soricidae)
    . . . *Suncus murinus*

Body covered with carapace of spines
Tail reduced to a short stump; ears large
Zygomatic arches (cheekbones) of skull complete (Fig. 2)
Large first upper incisor tooth simple, without rear cusp (Fig. 1)
. . . Hedgehogs (Erinaceidae)

    Spiny carapace uniformly coloured, tips of spines whitish throughout
    No naked gap between the spines on forehead
    Fur of underside pure white throughout
    . . . *Hemiechinus auritus*

    Spiny carapace with central blackish stripe, spines broadly white-tipped on flanks
    Naked gap between spines present on forehead
    Fur of underside mottled black and white
    . . . *Paraechinus aethiopicus*

    Spiny carapace uniformly blackish throughout
    Naked gap between spines present on forehead
    Fur of underside uniformly blackish, except for variable white speckling on chin
    . . . *Paraechinus hypomelas*

Fam. **Soricidae** (Shrews)

Suncus murinus   Indian house shrew
This large shrew is a rat-like animal with a short thickened tail. It is readily distinguished from a rodent by the long pointed snout, tiny eyes and small rounded ears. The fur is

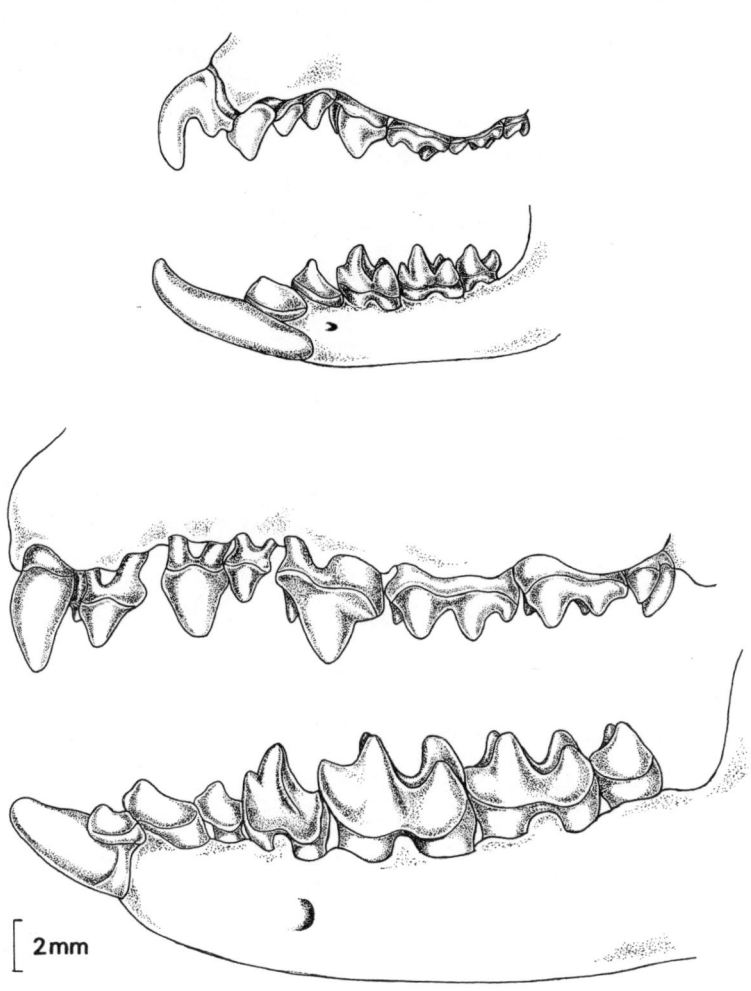

2mm

Fig. 1
Above: Dentition of the Indian House shrew (*Suncus murinus*)
Below: Dentition of the Ethiopian hedgehog (*Paraechinus aethiopicus*)
In shrews, the first upper incisor has two cusps; in hedgehogs it is a simple cone.

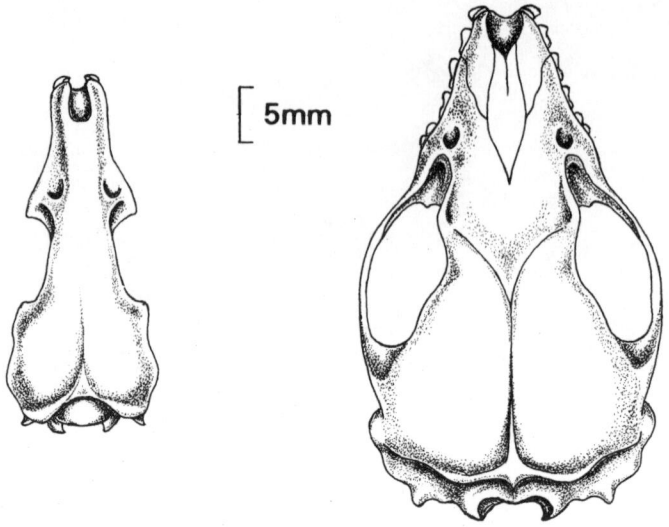

5mm

Fig. 2
Left: Skull of the Indian House shrew (*Suncus murinus*)
Right: Skull of the Ethiopian hedgehog (*Paraechinus aethiopicus*)
In shrews the zygomatic arches are missing; in hedgehogs they are complete.

short and close but the tail has long, scattered, whitish hairs projecting in a 'herring-bone' manner (Plate 1).

The species is commensal with man and has spread from its original homeland in the Orient through human agency. In Arabia it certainly arrived by sea and is consequently known only in the vicinity of seaports. It has been found not uncommonly in Bahrain Island where it is particularly numerous about refuse tips. Its diurnal activities, loud metallic squeaking and frequent presence around houses and gardens means that this species is often seen by man.

Measurements: total length 161–240 mm; tail 60–86 mm; hind foot 18–22 mm; ear 12–16 mm; greatest length of skull 29·0–35·0 mm.

Fam. **Erinaceidae** (Hedgehogs)

Hemiechinus auritus   Long-eared hedgehog
This is the smallest of the three handsome hedgehog species found in the region. Its very long ears, pure white belly, slender limbs and sandy-whitish spines and face combine to give it an elfin elegance somehow very suitable for the arid steppe desert that it inhabits (Plate 1).

It is essentially an inhabitant of the northern steppes and extends south along the rivers of Iraq as far as Kuwait. Like other hedgehogs it is strictly nocturnal and it finds shelter from the intense daytime heat in a well-constructed burrow. These little hedgehogs are remarkably aggressive to one another in captivity and probably remain solitary except in the breeding season.

Measurements: total length 153–223 mm; tail 13–37 mm; hind foot 28·3–35 mm; ear 29·8–43 mm; greatest length of skull 41·4–47·6 mm.

Paraechinus aethiopicus   Ethiopian hedgehog
This is a most elegant hedgehog. The blackish snout strongly contrasts with a white forehead band extending to the bases of the very large ears, while the whitish carapace is broadly banded with black down the spine and the belly is mottled black and white. The long slender legs enable it to run with surprising speed in the desert habitat to which it is so well adapted.

It is certainly the most abundant and widespread of the hedgehogs in desert Arabia and in the Gulf region it has been found in eastern Saudi Arabia, as well as in Ras al Khaima, near Buraimi and on Tanb Island. It is able to survive in extremely arid regions and, like many true desert species, must be largely water-independent. It is strictly nocturnal.

Measurements: total length 147–249 mm; tail 13–35 mm; hind foot 20–35 mm; ear 32·5–48 mm; greatest length of skull 43·8–52·2 mm.

Paraechinus hypomelas   Brandt's hedgehog

The Arabian form of this rare and rather little known species has been aptly called the Black hedgehog because of its uniformly blackish carapace and underside; only the face and chin are sparsely grizzled with white. Like the Ethiopian species the ears are very large, but narrower (Plate 1).

Its distribution suggests that it originally came to Arabia from Iran and southern Russia when these regions were connected across the Straits of Hormuz. It is still found on some islands in the Gulf and on the mainland it is a relict surviving in the high mountains of Oman and South Yemen. It has been found on Jebel Hafit and recently by M. D. Gallagher near Masafi and at Asimah in the UAE. It is also nocturnal with habits apparently similar to the other species, although little is known about its life in Arabia.

Measurements: total length 169–254 mm; tail 18–31·8 mm; hind foot 30–38 mm; ear 21–50·8 mm; greatest length of skull 45·7–52·3 mm.

Order **CHIROPTERA** (Bats)

Bats are the only mammals capable of true flight and, after more than sixty million years of evolution, have become one of the most highly adapted and specialised orders of mammals. They are readily distinguished from all other mammals by their wings, which are formed from greatly enlarged forelimbs, especially the forearms and fingers. They are covered by delicate membranes extending from the sides of the body and also enclosing the hind limbs and often the tail.

Both sub-orders of bats occur in this region: the Megachiroptera (fruit bats) contain only the one family, the Pteropodidae; while the Microchiroptera, with about twenty living families, are represented in the Arabian Gulf by five families: the Rhinopomatidae (mouse-tailed bats), the Emballonuridae (sheath-tailed bats), the Rhinolophidae (horseshoe bats), the Hipposideridae (leaf-nosed bats) and the Vespertilionidae (vespertilionid bats). A sixth family, the Molossidae (free-tailed bats), may well occur in the Gulf region, but has not yet been found there.

The Megachiroptera are in general larger and have large eyes, simple ears without tragi, and simple, longitudinally grooved cheekteeth; they possess a claw on the index finger, and the tail and tail membrane are usually very rudimentary (Fig. 3). They are mostly frugivorous and are confined to the tropical regions of the Old World.

The Microchiroptera have teeth with sharp cusps and ridges, and small eyes. Complex noseleaves are often developed and the ears are generally larger and more complex than those of the Megachiroptera – all evolved as part of their faculty of echolocation. The tail is usually well developed, and there is no index claw. Diet is generally insectivorous but in different species very varied to include

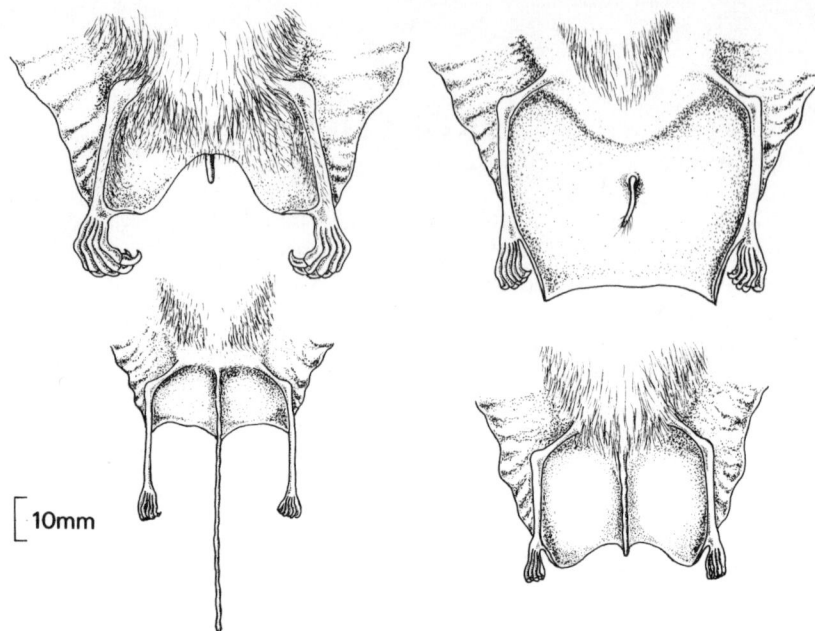

Fig. 3
The tail and its membrane in four families of Arabian bats.
Above left: *Rousettus aegyptiacus* (Pteropodidae)
Above right: *Taphozous nudiventris* (Emballonuridae)
Below left: *Rhinopoma muscatellum* (Rhinopomatidae)
Below right: *Rhinolophus clivosus* (Rhinolophidae)
In the Pteropodidae the tail is vestigial; in Emballonuridae it emerges through the upper surface of the large interfemoral membrane; in Rhinopomatidae the long tail is largely free from the short interfemoral membrane; in Rhinolophidae the tail is enclosed in the membrane to its tip.

fruit, fish, flesh, blood and nectar. They are very widely distributed, and only absent from the treeless circumpolar regions.

Their nocturnal habits make bats hard to distinguish on the wing; the nine known species of the Gulf may be identified by the key given below. At least ten other species which may occur in the region, but which have not yet been found there, are not included in the key but are referred to briefly in the text.

Key to the Chiroptera (Bats) of the Arabian Gulf

Tail reduced to a vestigial stump, less than 20 mm long, not enclosed in the interfemoral membrane (Fig. 3).
Index finger armed with a claw on the front edge of the wing
. . . Fruit bats (Megachiroptera: Pteropodidae)
  . . . *Rousettus aegyptiacus*

Tail well developed, more than 20 mm long and at least partly enclosed in the interfemoral membrane.
Index finger without any claw.
. . . Microchiroptera

 Tail emerges from the middle of the dorsal surface of the interfemoral membrane (Fig. 3)
 No noseleaf; ears separate, with a club-shaped tragus (inner earlet)
 . . . Sheath-tailed bats (Emballonuridae)
  . . . *Taphozous nudiventris*

 Tail projects from border of interfemoral membrane, more than half its length projecting free (Fig. 3)
 Small simple triangular noseleaf present; ears joined across forehead, with tragus notched at its tip
 . . . Mouse-tailed bats (Rhinopomatidae)
  Size smaller, forearm 46·1–50·5 mm
  Nasal inflations and tympanic bullae of skull larger, the former visible when skull is viewed from below
  . . . *Rhinopoma muscatellum*
  Size larger, forearm 47·8–59·3 mm
  Nasal inflations and tympanic bullae smaller, the

former invisible when skull is viewed from below
. . . *Rhinopoma hardwickei*

Tail more or less completely enclosed in the inter-femoral membrane
Large complex noseleaf present, with single vertical projection (lancet) from upper border; ears separate with no tragus (inner earlet)
. . . Horseshoe bats (Rhinolophidae)
   . . . *Rhinolophus clivosus*

Tail more or less completely enclosed in the inter-femoral membrane
Large complex noseleaf present, with three vertical projections from upper border; ears separate with no tragus
. . . Leaf-nosed bats (Hipposideridae)
   Wing with a small transverse bony projection at the base of the last phalanx of the third finger
   Ears with a marked notch in inner border below tip
   . . . *Triaenops persicus*
   Wing without transverse bony projection at base of last phalanx of third finger
   Ears without notch in inner border below tip
   . . . *Asellia tridens*

Tail more or less completely enclosed in the inter-femoral membrane
No noseleaf present; ears separate, tragus (inner earlet) present
. . . Vesper bats (Vespertilionidae)
   Size small, forearm 29·6–36·2 mm
   Ears not grossly enlarged, about 10–13 mm from notch to tip
   . . . *Pipistrellus kuhli*
   Size large, forearm 61–66 mm
   Ears grossly enlarged, about 36–42 mm from notch to tip
   . . . *Otonycteris hemprichi*

Fam. **Pteropodidae** (Fruit-eating bats)

Rousettus aegyptiacus   Egyptian fruit bat
This is the largest bat found in the Gulf region, with a
forearm of about 90 mm (Plate 2). It is readily recognisable
by its vestigial tail, which is not included in the tail membrane. The latter is reduced to a narrow band along the
inner border of the legs. The presence of a claw on the
index finger on the wing is also characteristic. The eyes are
larger than in the Microchiroptera and the ears are simple
(Fig. 4). The greyish-brown fur is fine and soft, but longer
in the throat region of adult males.

The Egyptian fruit bat is essentially a cave-dwelling
species, inhabiting also dark ruins. Perhaps as a result it is
one of the few fruit bats to develop the faculty of echolocation, using ultrasound produced by rapid vibration of the
tongue between the palate and the floor of the mouth,
unlike the signals made in the voice-box (larynx) of the
Microchiroptera. Its frugivorous habits make it an economic nuisance in fruit-growing areas where colonies may

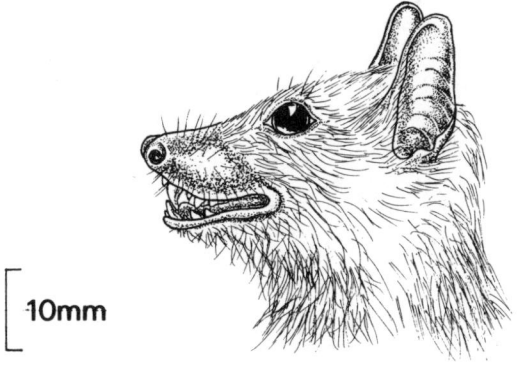

10mm

Fig. 4
Egyptian fruit bat (*Rousettus aegyptiacus*)
This species, a member of the Pteropodidae, has
large eyes, a rather dog-like face and simple ears,
without tragus.

ravage crops of bananas, dates, figs and other soft fruit. It is uncommon in the Gulf – suitable caverns are more or less confined to the Ras al-Khaimah peninsula (where M. D. Gallagher found a mummified specimen in 1972).

Measurements: total length 117–140 mm; tail 8–16 mm; forearm 81·2–94·1 mm; foot 17·2–22·8 mm; ear 18·2–20·8 mm; greatest length of skull 37·8–40·8 mm.

Fam. **Rhinopomatidae** (Mouse-tailed bats)

Rhinopoma muscatellum　　　　　Muscat mouse-tailed bat
This curious little bat is recognisable by its long, slender tail, most of which projects free from the tail membrane. The large ears are joined by a broad band across the forehead (Fig. 5); the tip of the tragus is slightly forked and the nose has a rather pig-like appearance, bearing a simple noseleaf. The greyish, fine hair does not extend to the lower belly or back.

Mouse-tailed bats inhabit dry caverns, rocky clefts and ruins, and may be distinguished on the wing by their curious rising and falling flight resembling that of a small bird. This species is more common in the Gulf region than *R. hardwickei;* it is not uncommon at Buraimi and in caves near Ras al-Khaimah.

Measurements: total length 101–117 mm; tail 46–63·5 mm; forearm 46·1–50·5 mm; foot 9–10·8 mm; ear 13·3–19·1 mm; greatest length of skull 15·1–16·1 mm.

Rhinopoma hardwickei　　　　　Lesser mouse-tailed bat
This species is scarcely distinguishable externally from the preceding one, although it is on average larger. Certain identification depends on examination of the skull, which has smaller tympanic bullae and nasal inflations, the latter invisible when the skull is viewed from below whereas in *R. muscatellum* they are clearly visible. Its habits are similar and it is included here since it has recently been found in eastern Saudi Arabia (Tuwayq Escarpment) by M. Jennings and it also occurs in Iraq.

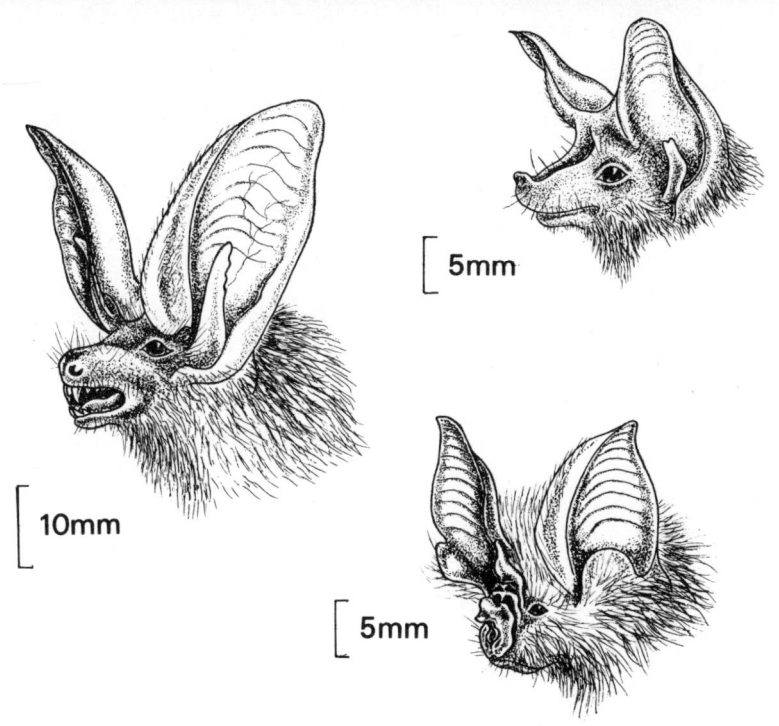

Fig. 5
Above: *Rhinopoma muscatellum* (Rhinopomatidae)
Centre: *Otonycteris hemprichi* (Vespertilionidae)
Below: *Rhinolophus clivosus* (Rhinolophidae)
In the Rhinopomatidae the ears are joined across the forehead, a tragus is present, notched at the tip and there is a small noseleaf. The Vespertilionidae have a simple muzzle, without noseleaf, and a large tragus. The Rhinolophidae have a complicated noseleaf and no tragus but a large antitragus.

Measurements: total length 93–137 mm; tail 45–79 mm; forearm 47·8–59·3 mm; foot 7–13·2 mm; greatest length of skull 16·1–19·6 mm.

A third species of Mouse-tailed bat, *Rhinopoma micro-*

phyllum, has occurred in Iran and northern parts of the Arabian peninsula and could probably also be found in the Gulf. It is the largest species in Arabia, with a forearm of 60–72 mm while the tail is usually shorter than the forearm.

Fam. **Emballonuridae** (Sheath-tailed bats)

Taphozous nudiventris   Naked-bellied tomb bat
The Naked-bellied tomb bat is a robust species with a forearm length of about 79 mm (Plate 2). It is at once recognisable by the tail, which emerges through the tail membrane at about the middle of its dorsal surface (Fig. 3). The muzzle is simple without any noseleaf and the ears contain a club-shaped tragus. The long narrow wings have a peculiar pocket formed by a fold of skin on the underside of the wrist stretching between the radius and fifth meta-carpal bones. The greyish-brown fur is soft and short but the lower belly is quite naked, from which the species' name is derived. A crescent-shaped fold of skin on the throat marks the position of a gular gland.

This is a colonial species living in large groups in rock crevices, ruins and sometimes the roofs of houses. The densely packed colonies emit a pungent, musky odour. The bats emerge at dusk and fly high with a powerful swift flight, making loud metallic squeaking noises. The Naked-bellied tomb bat probably occurs throughout the Gulf region, where it is represented by a large sub-species, *T. n. magnus,* on Bahrain Island, while the smaller *T. n. zayidi* has been found at Jebel Faiyah.

Measurements: total length 101–146 mm; tail 19–41 mm; forearm 64·9–82·5 mm; foot 11·3–22 mm; ear 18·7–25 mm; greatest length of skull 24·8–31·8 mm.

A second species of Tomb bat, *Taphozous perforatus,* has occurred on the Batinah Coast of Oman and could well be found in the Gulf: its external appearance is similar but without the naked belly and it is much smaller, the forearm being 61·3–65·3 mm.

Fam. **Rhinolophidae** (Horseshoe bats)

Rhinolophus clivosus   Arabian horseshoe bat
This bat derives its name from the large noseleaf covering
the muzzle, of which the lower part is shaped like a
horseshoe (Fig. 5). The upper portion of the leaf is composed of a single vertical lancet distinguishing this family
from the leaf-nosed bats of the Hipposideridae. A third
central part of the leaf which projects forwards is called the
sella because of its saddle-like appearance. In this species
its upper part (superior connecting process) is rounded in
side view. The Horseshoe bat has tall pointed ears, which
lack any tragus, but the antitragal lobe at the base of the
outer border is large. *R. clivosus* is a medium-sized bat, the
forearm being about 48 mm; it has long, soft, greyish hair
and the tail (enclosed in its membrane except for the extreme tip) reaches to the feet when extended.

It is a colonial species living in caves, dark cellars and
ruins, where its highly developed powers of echolocation
enable it to fly in pitch darkness. It is not common in the
Arabian Gulf, but is included here as it occurs in eastern
Saudi Arabia, where Michael Jennings recently found it at
the Tuwayq Escarpment.

Measurements: total length 77–93 mm; tail 19·6–38 mm;
forearm 45·6–52·1 mm; foot 6·9–10·3 mm; ear 18–21·8
mm; greatest length of skull 19·8–21·2 mm.

Another species of Horseshoe bat, *Rhinolophus blasii,* has
recently been found on the Batinah Coast of Oman and
may occur in this region. It is similar in size and general
appearance to the Arabian horseshoe bat, but the upper
part of the sella is acutely pointed in side view instead of
being low and rounded.

Fam. **Hipposideridae** (Leaf-nosed bats)

Asellia tridens   Trident leaf-nosed bat
The Trident bat has a more complex noseleaf covering the

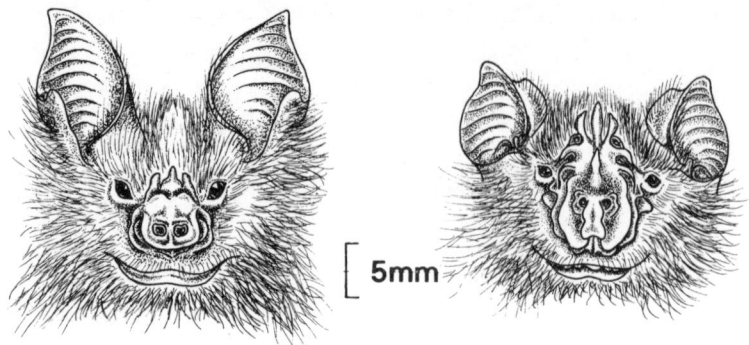

Fig. 6
Left: Trident leaf-nosed bat (*Asellia tridens*)
Right: Persian leaf-nosed bat (*Triaenops persicus*)
Both these species are members of the Hipposideridae (leaf-nosed bats). Both have three vertical spikes on the top of the noseleaf, but in *Triaenops* the leaf is much more complex. The ears of *Asellia* are tall and pointed, but in *Triaenops* the shorter ears have a deep notch in their front edges.

muzzle than that of the Horseshoe bat; there is no central projection as there is on the Horseshoe bat and the horseshoe round the nostrils is surrounded on its outside edge by leaflets (secondary folioles) (Fig. 6). The ears are tall and pointed like the Horseshoe bat, similarly lacking a tragus, and the long fur is pale greyish-white; about 5 mm of the tail tip projects from the membrane. It is also a medium-sized bat, with the forearm being about 48 mm.

Trident bats are colonial, roosting in caverns, ruins and often in the narrow underground tunnels of the water falaj systems. Their flight is low and butterfly-like, their pale colour imparting a ghostly quality as they flit about the oases and gardens at dusk. *A. tridens* is one of the most widespread and abundant of the Arabian bats, occurring wherever there are suitable roosts in the region.

Measurements: total length 61–85 mm; tail 16–27 mm; forearm 43·5–52·4 mm; foot 5–9·5 mm; ear 14–22 mm; greatest length of skull 17·1–19·2 mm.

40

Triaenops persicus   Persian leaf-nosed bat
This extraordinary little bat must surely rank as one of the
most fascinating small mammals in the world. Like that of
the Trident bat, the muzzle is covered by a noseleaf with
three vertical processes, but in this case it is far more
complex: a fourth small vertical projection stands at the
base of the middle one, elaborate folds are developed
around and between the nostrils and there are also secondary folioles and pockets surrounding the leaf (Fig. 6). The
precise function of this complex structure is unknown. The
ears are smaller than those of the Trident bat and have a
peculiar notch in their front edges below the tips. In the
wing a thin spike of bone projects into the membrane from
the base of the last phalanx of the third finger – a unique
feature. The fur is soft and fine, with pale orange and
greyish colour variants.

It is a colonial species with habits rather similar to the
Trident bat but it is much scarcer in the Gulf region. It was
found by the author in the water falaj tunnels at Al Ain, in
the Buraimi Oasis.

Measurements: total length 79·7–88·2 mm; tail 25–31·8
mm; forearm 47·1–51·6 mm; foot 7·2–10·5 mm; ear 10·8–
14·6 mm; greatest length of skull 18·2–19·7 mm.

Fam. **Vespertilionidae** (Vespertilionid bats)

Pipistrellus kuhli   Kuhl's pipistrelle
In all the 'vesper' bats of this family the muzzle is simple,
without any noseleaf, and yet the external ear does contain
a tragus. This is the smallest bat in the region, with a
forearm length of about 33 mm. The short fur is pale clay-
brown and the wing and tail membranes are pale and
translucent. The overall small size and in particular the
small ears distinguish this bat from the following species.

Kuhl's pipistrelle is colonial, often found in crevices in
the walls of buildings and is the commonest bat to be seen
flying around the houses and gardens of the Gulf region at

dusk. It has been found in numerous localities and occurs in all of the Arabian Gulf countries.

Measurements: total length 65–93 mm; tail 29–40·5 mm; forearm 29·6–36·2 mm; foot 5–8 mm; ear 10–14·5 mm; greatest length of skull 12·2–14·0 mm.

Otonycteris hemprichi   Hemprich's long-eared bat
These are large bats with the forearm measuring about 62 mm. They are recognisable by their very large ears with tall and pointed tragi (Fig. 5). The pale, greyish-white fur gives these bats a ghostly appearance. Only the tail tip projects from the membrane and the male phallus is peculiar in form, resembling a boot projecting from a boxing glove.

This is a rare species in the region. It occurs at the Hofuf Oasis and recently some skulls were found in the pellets of birds of prey in a cave near Ras al-Khaimah by M. D. Gallagher. It is apparently well adapted to desert life, inhabiting caves, rock crevices and occasionally buildings. Its flight is slow and floppy but little is known about its habits.

Measurements: total length 101–188 mm; tail 40–58 mm; forearm 57–66 mm; foot 10–14 mm; ear 31·5–42 mm; greatest length of skull 20·8–24·9 mm.

Some other species of bat have occurred in neighbouring parts of Arabia, but have not as yet been found in the Gulf region. They include *Tadarida aegyptiaca, Myotis emarginatus, Eptesicus bottae, Eptesicus walli, Eptesicus nasutus, Pipistrellus rüppelli* and *Pipistrellus arabicus.* These species could possibly occur there but recognition is not always easy and usually requires an examination of the technical details of the skull and teeth. Such details are given in *The Mammals of Arabia* (Vol. I).

Order **CARNIVORA** (Carnivores)

This order includes seven families, most of which (like dogs and cats) are specialised for hunting live prey and eating flesh; others (like bears and raccoons) are omnivorous, while some are scavengers or even insectivores.

Sizes vary from the small animals such as weasels to the massive Brown and Polar bears. Most carnivores are terrestrial, although a few are aquatic or semi-aquatic and some are arboreal. The brain of a carnivore has well developed cerebral hemispheres with convolutions; the digits – at least four on each foot – are always clawed. A baculum (penis-bone) is usually present. The carnivorous habits of most members are reflected in the teeth; they are distinguishable from other placental mammals by the presence of a specially modified flesh-tooth (carnassial) in each jaw. The canine teeth are usually powerful as well.

Five families from the order occur in the Gulf region. The Canidae (dogs) are specialised for the terrestrial pursuit and capture of prey, they have long limbs, run on their toes and have well-developed tympanic bullae and carnassials. The Mustelidae are slender, short-limbed animals of small or moderate size, specialised for terrestrial life (like weasels), or fossorial (like badgers), or arboreal (like martens), or even aquatic (like otters). Carnassial teeth are well developed; the tympanic bullae are rather flat and lack a septum; and the skull sutures fuse early in life. The Viverridae (mongooses and genets) are rather similar in build to the Mustelids, with slender bodies and short limbs, but the tympanic bullae are inflated and divided by a septum into two chambers. Moreover, they differ in some dental details. The Hyaenidae (hyaenas) are scavengers, with long slender legs and hindquarters which are noticeably lower than the forequarters. The skull has a deep braincase, a strong crest on the skull vault and carries short, powerful jaws. The dentition is highly specialised for cracking bones, the upper carnassial being exceptionally powerful. The Felidae (cats), which hunt by stealth, have slender bodies, are moderate to large in size and have digits armed with powerful claws which are retractable into sheaths, except in the case of the cheetah (*Acinonyx*). The cheekteeth are strictly ridged and cuspidate, without crushing surfaces, and with highly developed carnassials.

The thirteen species known to occur in the Gulf region are identified in the key given below. Four other species which may possibly be found are mentioned briefly in the text.

Key to the Carnivora (Carnivores) of the Arabian Gulf

Legs short and stocky, body slender; tympanic bullae flattened; cranial sutures fused early in life (Fig. 7)
    . . . Mustelids (Mustelidae)

> 32 teeth in all; back of body from crown of head is white; with contrasting black colouring of underside, snout, limbs and tail tip
>   . . . *Mellivora capensis*

Legs longer and more slender; tympanic bullae swollen; cranial sutures fused only when adult

> 42 teeth in all; skull elongated; four to five toes on the fore feet and four on the hindfeet.
>   . . . Dogs (Canidae)

>> Frontal region of skull prominent, swollen with air cells:
>> Size very large; hind foot 184–197 mm; greatest length of skull 184·5–238 mm; upper molars lacking well-defined cingulum
>>   . . . *Canis lupus*
>> Size smaller; hind foot 140–170 mm; greatest length of skull 138–176 mm; upper molars with a

well-developed cingulum
. . . *Canis aureus*

Frontal region of skull flattened, not swollen with air cells:
Larger, hind foot 100–150 mm; greatest length of skull 110–145 mm; ears with black or dusky tips; teeth normal
. . . *Vulpes vulpes*

Smaller, hind foot 90–115 mm; greatest length of skull 97–109 mm; ears without black or dusky tips; teeth normal
. . . *Vulpes rüppelli*

Smallest, hind foot 92–98 mm; greatest length of

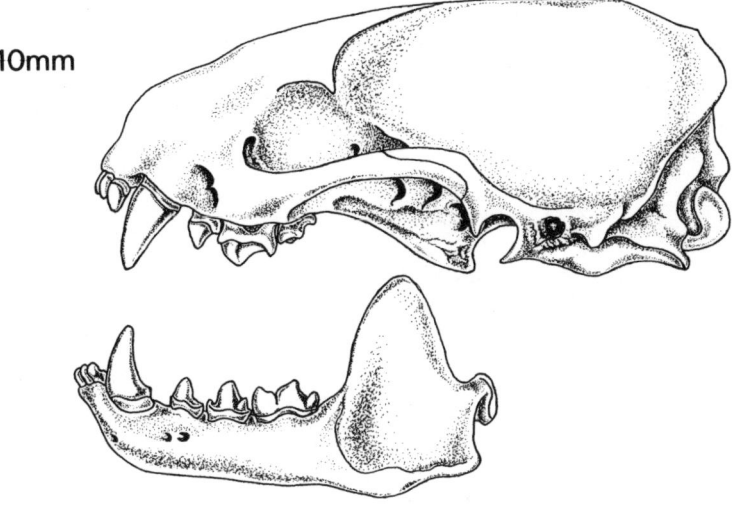

10mm

Fig. 7
Skull of the Honey badger (*Mellivora capensis*). In *Mellivora*, a member of the Mustelidae, the cranial sutures are fused early in life and the tympanic bullae are flattened. The teeth normally number 32, but in this specimen from South Yemen the front upper and lower premolars are lacking.

45

skull 80–87 mm; ears without black or dusky tips, teeth feeble.

. . . *Fennecus zerda*

40 teeth in all; skull elongated; four or five toes on front and hind feet

. . . Mongooses (Viverridae)

Medium in size; total length 710–740 mm; coloration coarsely speckled olive grey-brown; tympanic bullae with rear chamber much more inflated than front one (Fig. 8)

. . . *Herpestes edwardsi*

34 teeth in all; skull short and broad at zygomatic arches; braincase flattened from sides; only four toes on front and hind feet

. . . Hyaenas (Hyaenidae)

Build heavy; dog-like; with pronounced vertical striped pattern and dorsal mane

. . . *Hyaena hyaena*

30 teeth or less in all; skull short and broad; five toes on front and four on hind feet

. . . Cats (Felidae)

Small cats (greatest length of skull 80–99 mm): Tympanic bullae not grossly enlarged, 18–23 mm. maximum diameter; without pronounced black elbow bars; ears small

. . . *Felis silvestris*

Tympanic bullae grossly inflated, 25 mm or more maximum diameter (Fig. 9); with pronounced black elbow bars; ears very large

. . . *Felis margarita*

Medium-sized cats (greatest length of skull 110–130 mm):

Body uniformly coloured, no pattern; long ear tufts

. . . *Caracal caracal*

Large cats (greatest length of skull 166–245 mm):

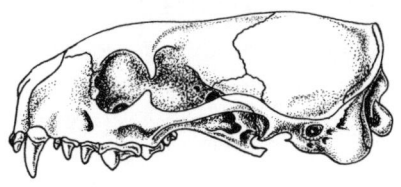

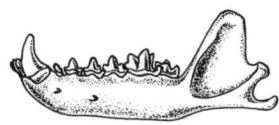

Fig. 8
Skull of the Indian grey mongoose (*Herpestes edwardsi ferrugineus*). In *Herpestes,* a member of the Viverridae, there are 40 teeth in all and the skull is elongated; the tympanic bulla is composed of two chambers, of which the rear one is much more inflated.

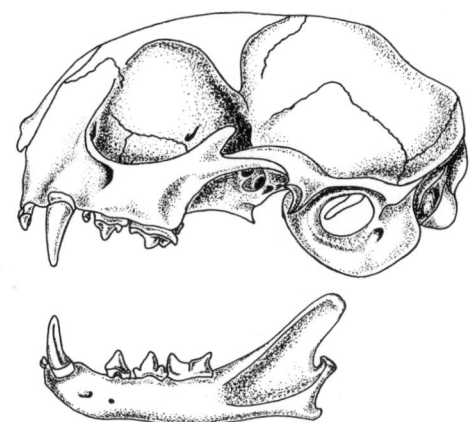

Fig. 9
Skull of the Arabian sand cat (*Felis margarita harrisoni*). The Sand cat, a member of the Felidae, has a domed skull with very short facial part. The teeth, adapted for cutting and piercing, number only 30 and the tympanic bullae are greatly inflated in this remarkable desert predator.

47

Spots on body form hollow rosettes; no black
stripes from eyes to mouth
. . . *Panthera pardus*
Spots on body are all solid; black stripes from
eyes to mouth
. . . *Acinonyx jubatus*

Fam. **Mustelidae** (Mustelids)

Mellivora capensis   Honey badger
The Honey badger, or Ratel as it is sometimes called, is
one of the most distinctive of the Arabian mammals due to
its unique coloration (Plate 3). The black of the underside,
the limbs, the snout and the tail tip contrasts sharply with
the white of the back, the crown of the head and the tail
base. The build is heavy, the limbs are short and the
forefeet are armed with massive claws.

The distinctive coloration undoubtedly has a warning
function, for this animal defends itself not only with a
powerful bite, but also with a nauseating secretion from
special skunk-like anal glands. It is an omnivorous carnivore, active both in daylight and at night. In Arabia it can
exist in very arid regions, feeding largely on lizards which it
excavates from their burrows. Its fondness for honey has
been observed elsewhere in its wide African and Asiatic
range, and like the Hyaena, it has even been blamed for the
disinterment of human corpses. In the Gulf region it can be
found from the vicinity of Kuwait down into the eastern
coastal regions of Saudi Arabia.

Measurements: total length 788–927 mm; tail 190–246
mm; hind foot 101·5–108 mm; ear 27–34·5 mm; greatest
length of skull 126 mm.

Fam. **Canidae** (Dogs, jackals, wolves and foxes)

Canis lupus   Wolf
Although the Arabian wolf (*C. l. arabs*) is considerably
smaller than its northern Eurasian relatives, it is neverthe-

PLATE 1
a   Long-eared hedgehog *(Hemiechinus auritus)*
b   Ethiopian hedgehog *(Paraechinus aethiopicus)*
c   Brandt's hedgehog *(Paraechinus hypomelas)*
d   Indian house shrew *(Suncus murinus)*

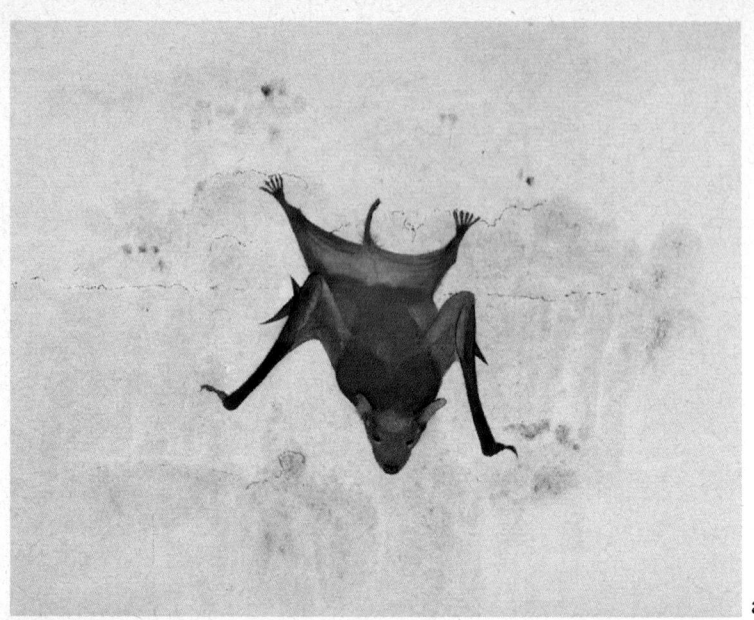

a

b

PLATE 2
a   Naked-bellied tomb bat *(Taphozous nudiventris)*
b   Egyptian fruit bat *(Rousettus aegyptiacus)*

a

b

PLATE 3
a   Honey badger *(Mellivora capensis)*
b   Indian grey mongoose *(Herpestes edwardsi ferrugineus)*

a

b

PLATE 4
a Arabian wolf *(Canis lupus arabs)*
b Striped hyaena *(Hyaena hyaena)*

a

b

PLATE 5
a Asiatic jackal *(Canis aureus)*
b Common red fox *(Vulpes vulpes)*

PLATE 6
a   Arabian sand cat *(Felis margarita harrisoni)*
b   Fennec fox *(Fennecus zerda)*

a

b

PLATE 7
a   Caracal lynx *(Caracal caracal)*
b   Wild cat *(Felis silvestris tristrami)*

PLATE 8
a   Asiatic cheetah *(Acinonyx jubatus venaticus)*
b   Arabian leopard *(Panthera pardus nimr)*

a

b

PLATE 9
a   Arabian tahr *(Hemitragus jayakari)*
b   Arabian oryx *(Oryx leucoryx)*

a

b

PLATE 10
a   Arabian goitred gazelle *(Gazella subgutturosa
marica)*
b   Arabian gazelle *(Gazella gazella arabica)*

a

b

PLATE 11
a   Indian crested porcupine *(Hystrix indica)*
b   Cape hare *(Lepus capensis)*

PLATE 12
a   Euphrates jerboa *(Allactaga euphratica)*
b   Arabian lesser jerboa *(Jaculus jaculus
vocator)*

less strikingly larger than the Jackal, with a total length of about 1140 mm. The general build is like an Alsatian dog, with rather long legs, a short, bushy tail and large ears (Plate 4). The coat is rather short and coarse, variably greyish or yellowish brown on the flanks, with a blackish crest along the spine. The tip of the tail is also black, while the cheeks and underside are usually white. Wolves from the more northerly parts of the peninsula (*C. l. pallipes*) are larger and have thicker, more luxuriant coats.

The desert wolves of Arabia usually hunt singly or in pairs, and many tales are told by the Beduin of their cunning in snatching sheep from the flocks. Considering the long-standing enmity of the species with man it is surprising that young wolves can be readily tamed. The species seems to be dependent on water and is therefore not found in the hearts of the deserts. It has occurred, albeit in scanty numbers, throughout the Gulf region from Dibbah, Buraimi and Jebel Hafit in the south to Hofuf, Jabrin and the vicinity of Kuwait in the north.

Measurements: total length 1140 mm; tail 320 mm; hind foot 184–197 mm; ear 80–92 mm; greatest length of skull 184·5–220 mm.

Canis aureus   Asiatic jackal

The general appearance of the Asiatic jackal is similar to the Wolf, but it is considerably smaller and differs in some features of the skull and teeth. Its hair is shaggy and its colour variable: generally brown with black speckling on its back, and white ventrally. The Asiatic jackal does not have a defined black spinal mane and the tail is strongly variegated in black, white and tan brown (Plate 5).

Jackals roam in packs and, like the Wolf, they are nocturnal or crepuscular, their dismal howling often audible around human settlements as they scavenge for food. In daytime they hide in dense thickets or, again like wolves, in caverns or rocky clefts. They have been found in the vicinity of Hofuf, but do not seem to be numerous south of Iraq and are altogether absent from Oman.

Measurements: total length 825–1015 mm; tail 210–270 mm; hind foot 147–162 mm; ear 58–89 mm; greatest length of skull 139–163·6 mm.

Vulpes vulpes   Common red fox
The Red fox is the most widespread Arabian carnivore. It can be distinguished from the other foxes of the region by its larger size and by the distinctive black or dusky outer ear tips (Plate 5). The build is generally more slender than the preceding canids and the tail is longer and more bushy. The tympanic bullae are notably smaller than those of the specialised desert foxes below. It is a most versatile predator, ranging widely in the Palearctic region and throughout the whole Arabian peninsula except the hearts of the sand deserts. Dwelling in burrows, rock crevices and caverns, the fox is a predominantly nocturnal hunter with rather omnivorous tastes; its usual diet of small birds, mammals and reptiles may be augmented at times by fruit and insects.
    Measurements: total length 607–920 mm; tail 240–380 mm; hind foot 100–137·5 mm; ear 67–109 mm; greatest length of skull 113·8–145 mm.

Vulpes rüppelli   Rüppell's sand fox
This elegant desert fox is smaller than the Red fox and has strikingly larger ears, of which the outer tips lack any black colour. It is not infrequently mistaken for the Fennec fox, which is in fact considerably smaller and has even larger ears. The fur is soft and silky and pale in hue, and the tympanic bullae are strikingly larger than those of the Red fox. The tail tip is usually white.
    V. rüppelli is apparently confined to the sand deserts of the interior and even there it is scarce (Michael Gallagher found a skull near Jebel Ali, Dubai, in 1973). A female from the Oman–Abu Dhabi frontier region was recently received from Peter Dickinson. Little is known about its habits in Arabia, where it is believed to subsist mainly on small desert mammals and birds.

Measurements: total length 593–805 mm; tail 260–355 mm; hind foot 90–112 mm; ear 88–110 mm; greatest length of skull 91·1–109·2 mm.

Fennecus zerda   Fennec fox
This is the smallest and scarcest desert fox in Arabia. It is identifiable by its very large, uniformly coloured ears, pale coat with black tail tip (Plate 6), very large tympanic bullae and degenerate teeth.

The Fennec fox is known mainly from the deserts of North Africa, and there are very few confirmed Arabian records (one of which came from the desert of Kuwait). It dwells in sandy deserts and in spite of its specialised habits has been successfully kept in captivity. It utters a bark like that of a small domestic dog.

Measurements: total length 583 mm; tail 215 mm; hind foot 96 mm; ear 97 mm; greatest length of skull 80–87 mm.

Fam. **Viverridae** (Mongooses, genets)

Herpestes edwardsi   Indian grey mongoose
The Indian grey mongoose is distinguishable from the other carnivores of the Gulf region by its long, slender form and rather uniform, coarsely speckled, olive-grey/brown coat. The cheeks, underparts, ears and tail tip often have a rusty orange tinge. The long tail is bushy, but tapered towards the tip; the ears are low and rounded (Plate 3). The elongated skull has the rear chamber of the tympanic bulla greatly enlarged.

The species lives around houses and gardens and like most other mongooses it is diurnal and omnivorous – feeding on fish, eggs and small vertebrates. It is essentially an Oriental species reaching its most western limit in the Arabian Gulf littoral, where it has occurred at Kuwait and south to 'Uqair, Sayhat and Bahrain Island.

Measurements: total length 711–739 mm; tail 305–371 mm; hind foot 69–70 mm; ear 12–18 mm; greatest length of skull 70–77 mm.

51

Fam. **Hyaenidae** (Hyaenas)

Hyaena hyaena   Striped hyaena

The Striped hyaena is unmistakeable amongst Arabian carnivores on account of its striped coat, pronounced dorsal mane and heavy dog-like build with relatively low hindquarters (Plate 4). The massive carnassial teeth and deep, narrow braincase are also characteristic. The specialised glandular pouch above the anus has led to the mistaken belief that the hyaena changes its sex annually.

It is a nocturnal animal, living in caves or earth dens and feeding largely on carrion. It has an unsavoury reputation for disinterring human corpses. Powerful teeth enable the hyaena to break up large bones. It is distributed across northern Africa and India, has been found near Safa in Summan and is certainly more widespread in the Gulf region than the few confirmed records suggest.

Measurements: total length 1450 mm; tail 295 mm; hind foot 220 mm; ear 150 mm; greatest length of skull 233–251·8 mm.

Fam. **Felidae** (Cats)

Felis silvestris   Wild cat

The Wild cat is small in size and can be distinguished externally from the equally small Sand cat, *Felis margarita,* by its smaller ears and absence of pronounced black elbow bars (Plate 7). The tympanic bullae are relatively small, about 18–23 mm in diameter. The general colour is tawny or ash-grey with an indistinct pattern on the body; the ears are rusty brown on their backs; the underside is whitish or buff.

The Wild cat is a nocturnal predator, feeding on small vertebrates as well as insects and favouring rocky habitats and bushy scrub country. It is an extremely agile climber. The Wild cat is widely distributed throughout Eurasia and Africa and in the Gulf it is unlikely to be as scarce as the few records suggest. A pale desert sub-species, *F. s. iraki,* is known in the desert of Kuwait, while the darker sub-species *F. s. tristrami,* has been found at Dubai.

Measurements: total length 669–888 mm; tail 263–390 mm; hind foot 110·2–131 mm; ear 55–67 mm; greatest length of skull 82·7–99 mm.

Felis margarita   Sand cat
This is also a small species, but distinguishable from the Wild cat by its much larger ears and pronounced elbow bars (Plate 6). The soles of the feet are covered by long tufts of hair and the tympanic bullae are very large (25 mm or more in diameter). The colour is a very pale sand-yellow (with faint markings) on the upper body, the tail is ringed with black and the ear tips are also black while the under-side and the feet are white.

The Sand cat is a mammal specially adapted for life in sandy deserts. The dense mat of hairs on the feet helps its grip when it is moving in the sand dunes. It digs a burrow in the sand to shelter from the intense heat and, like the Wild cat, it is a nocturnal hunter. It ranges from the deserts of North Africa through Arabia to Iran, Russian Turkestan and Baluchistan. The Arabian sub-species (*F.m. harrisoni*) is still known only in a few localities: one was found in eastern Saudi Arabia between As Sarrar and Al 'Uwaynah and it is also known to exist in the Qatar–Abu Dhabi frontier area.

Measurements: total length 702–740 mm; tail 250–300 mm; hind foot 110 mm; ear 57–68 mm; greatest length of skull 86·5–90·3 mm.

Caracal caracal   Caracal lynx
This is a medium-sized cat, at once distinguishable from other Arabian cats by its uniform reddish/sandy colour without any pattern on the body (Plate 7). Long black and white ear tufts are present in the adults and a prominent black spot can usually be seen above the eye.

The Caracal inhabits arid steppe and mountain terrain, where its sandy coat blends admirably with the rocky environment. It lives in rock crevices and caverns and is very secretive. It is a powerful and agile hunter with great jumping power and it has been credited with the ability to catch flying birds in its paws. It ranges widely from South Africa to India and in the Gulf region it has been found at Tawi Suwaihan, north-west of Buraimi.

Measurements: total length 857 mm; tail 227 mm; hind foot 157 mm; ear 74 mm; greatest length of skull 110·3–129·1 mm.

Panthera pardus   Leopard

This large and formidable cat has a distinctive pattern with the spots on its body forming hollow rosettes (Plate 8). Unlike that of the Cheetah, its face lacks the prominent black stripe extending from each eye to the mouth. The massive claws have complete sheaths. The Arabian sub-species *P.p. nimr* is small by comparison and the background colour between the spots is pale, almost white.

The Leopard is confined to mountains and hilly terrain. The damage it causes to domestic animal stocks and its occasional attacks on humans have rendered it a long-standing enemy of mankind. As a result of its secretive habits and choice of lairs in remote mountain fastnesses, it has fared better than the Cheetah in the struggle to survive in a hostile world. Nevertheless, in the Gulf region it is known only in the mountains of the Ras al-Khaimah peninsula. Elsewhere, the species has a wide range from Africa, through Arabia and Asia Minor, to the Caucasus, Iran and Turkestan, and eastwards to India and parts of the Far East.

Measurements: total length 1600–2007 mm; tail 660–814 mm; ear 44 mm; greatest length of skull 166·3–208 mm.

Acinonyx jubatus   Cheetah

The Cheetah is another large cat, distinguishable from the Leopard by the pattern of solid spots on the body and by the presence of a prominent black stripe from each eye to the mouth (Plate 8). In addition, the claws lack complete sheaths. The long, slender limbs are well suited to the swift pursuit of prey, and this is the Cheetah's special skill.

Unlike the Leopard, it is an inhabitant of open plains, relying on its amazing speed over short distances to overtake and capture animals such as gazelles and hares. Distributed at one time from Africa, through Arabia, to Iran, Turkestan and India, it has now become very scarce in much of this territory and it may already be extinct in the Gulf region, where it has in the past been recorded in the area of Kuwait.

Measurements: Greatest length of skull 172 mm.

Two other species of mongoose have occurred in neighbouring parts of the peninsula: the White-tailed mongoose, *Ichneumia albicauda* (essentially an African species) occurs in Oman, and the small Indian mongoose, *Herpestes auropunctatus,* is found in Iraq. Two species of otter also occur in southern Iraq: the Common otter, *Lutra lutra,* and the Indian smooth-coated otter, *Lutra perspicillata.* These carnivores could possibly be found in the Gulf region.

Order **ARTIODACTYLA** (Even-toed Ungulates)

The hoofed mammals belonging to this order are mainly distinguished by the structure of the foot. In almost all cases this has an even number of well-developed digits, with the main axis of the limb passing between the third and fourth digit. In some forms the central wrist or ankle bones are fused to form cannon bones and the lateral wrist or ankle bones and digits may be vestigial or absent. Varying in size from tiny mouse deer to the large giraffes, the nine living families are distributed throughout the globe except for Australia, New Zealand, Antarctica and some remote islands. The order has furnished man with some of his most important domesticated mammals. The upper incisors are small or absent in artiodactyls and canine teeth are generally lost, but may be developed as tusk-like weapons. There is usually a long space (diastema) between the front teeth and the cheekteeth. The latter are more or less specialised for chewing vegetation and may be low-crowned and cuspidate or high-crowned with crescentic ridges, as in the ruminants ('cud-chewers') in which the stomach is particulary complicated. Horns or antlers are developed in some families.

Six wild species of the Bovidae, which include cattle, goats, sheep and antelopes, occur in this region. They may be identified by use of the key given below. Three other species which could possibly occur are briefly mentioned in the text.

Key to the Artiodactyla (Even-toed ungulates) of the Arabian Gulf

Horns of adult male very long, more than 360 mm base to

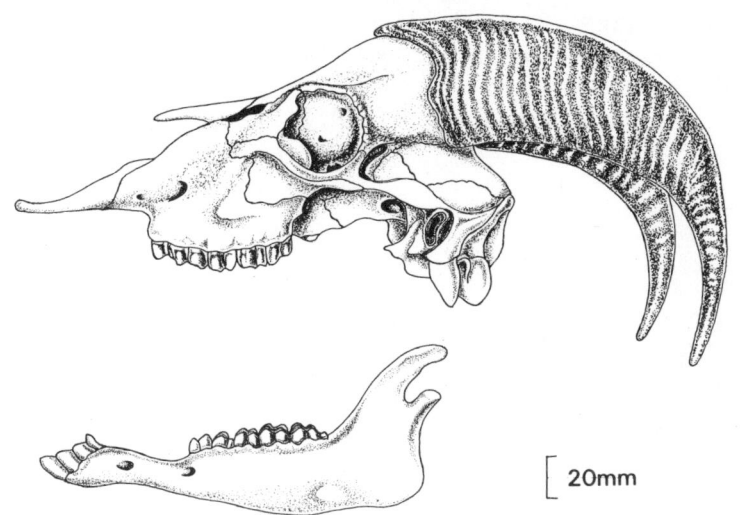

Fig. 10
Skull of the Arabian tahr (*Hemitragus jayakari*).
The tahr, a member of the Bovidae, has a long
diastema and absent upper incisors as in most
Artiodactyla. The horns of the adult male, shown
here, are short, curved and compressed from the
sides, with a smooth front edge. They are never
shed.

tip, curved like a scimitar with irregular longitudinal knobs
on anterior keel; those of female much smaller
Adult male with prominent beard
Wrists and ankles with prominent black and white pattern;
no ruffs on legs in winter coat
  . . . *Capra aegagrus*

Horns of adult male short, not more than about 260 mm
from their bases in front to their tip, keels in front smooth,
curved less strongly to a semi-circle (Fig. 10); those of the
female not outstandingly smaller
Adult male without beard
Wrists and ankles without contrasting black and white
pattern; prominent ruffs on legs in winter coat
  . . . *Hemitragus jayakari*

57

Adult horns of both sexes very long (500–710 mm from their bases in front to their tips), only slightly curved backwards, circular in section with rings at bases
Colour of adult white with contrasting dark markings on face, horn bases, middle of chest, front of legs and tail tip
Large antelope (greatest length of skull about 248–312 mm)

   . . . *Oryx leucoryx*

Horns of adult male shorter (not exceeding about 315 mm), oval in section, with more or less marked S-shaped curvature, ringed nearly to tips
Colour of back pale brown, white below with variably developed flank, facial and gluteal stripes
Size small and build slender (greatest length of skull not exceeding about 210 mm)

   . . . Gazelles (*Gazella*)

Horns of adult male long (210–313 mm), widely divergent at tips and lyre-shaped; close together at bases (gap usually less than 13 mm)
Adult females may be hornless or with slender horns up to 220 mm long
Male with a goitre-like throat swelling; build thickset; face usually whitish with facial, flank and gluteal stripes obsolete

   . . . *Gazella subgutturosa*

Horns of adult male long (265–310 mm), less widely divergent at tips and straight; wider apart at bases (gap usually about 13 mm)
Adult female horns long (175–240 mm), slender and nearly straight
Nasal bones overlap posterior extremities of the premaxillae, with a long junction; width of nasals usually greatest distally
Build light, with short legs
Colour light; flank stripe usually obsolete but facial stripes distinct

   . . . *Gazella dorcas*

Horns of adult male short (150–269 mm) with large gap at base (about 25 mm)
Horns of adult female short (85–135 mm)
Nasal bones scarcely overlap posterior extremities of premaxillae, with a short junction; nasal width usually greatest proximally
Build slender, with long legs
Colour darker, facial, flank and gluteal stripes usually well-defined
   . . . *Gazella gazella*

Fam. **Bovidae** (Cattle, goats, sheep, antelopes)

Capra aegagrus   Wild goat

The Wild goat is recognisable by the long horns of the adult male, each curved like a scimitar and with irregular longitudinal knobs on the anterior keel. The male has a prominent beard and a well-marked colour pattern, with a dark spinal stripe, an additional stripe across the shoulders and flank stripes from the axillae to the groins; both sexes have strongly contrasting black and white markings on the wrists and ankles. Females have fainter markings and considerably smaller horns.

The species ranges from the Greek Islands through southern Asia Minor, Iran, the northern Arabian peninsula and the Caucasus east to Baluchistan, Sind, southern Russian Turkmenia and possibly Afghanistan. In the Gulf region, it has occurred only once in hills near Masafi, in the UAE, and there has been no further occurrence to confirm its existence in the mountains of eastern Arabia. It is essentially an inhabitant of rocky mountain ranges, where it is an agile climber like the closely related Ibex. It may be solitary or found in large herds. The 'bezoar' stone, formerly esteemed for its medicinal powers, is a concretion formed in the stomach of this animal.

Measurements: total length 1045–1200 mm; tail 110–130 mm; hind foot 257–312 mm; greatest length of skull 246 mm.

Hemitragus jayakari   Arabian tahr

The Arabian tahr is one of the most interesting indigenous mammals of the region. Adult males are beardless and have short, curved horns compressed from the sides; a blackish spinal crest is present, as is contrasted black and white facial striping (Plate 9). Both these latter characteristics are less marked in females, which have horns only slightly smaller than those of the male. In winter the shaggy coat forms tufts on the angles of the jaws and ruffs on the legs, but there is no contrasting black and white pattern on the wrists and ankles.

Although related species are found in the Indian peninsula, *H. jayakari* is confined to the mountain ranges of Oman and the UAE in eastern Arabia. In this region it is known only from an isolated population found by Wilfred Thesiger on Jebel Hafit, a massif isolated from the main range. It has become increasingly scarce in Oman, where the Government has established a special reserve to save this unique wild goat from extinction. Like the Wild goat, it is an inhabitant of mountain ranges, dwelling on precipitous cliffs and ledges and seeking shelter in shallow caves in the cliff face.

Measurements: total length 952 mm; tail 84 mm; ear 85–99 mm; greatest length of skull 201·2–219 m.

Oryx leucoryx   Arabian oryx

This elegant indigenous Arabian antelope is now unfortunately almost certainly extinct in the wild state, but has been saved from total extinction in captivity. It is at once recognisable by the very long horns, which are ringed at the base and only slightly curved backwards. The white background colour, contrasted with dark chocolate markings on the face, neck, limbs and tail tip, are also unlike any other Arabian mammal (Plate 9).

Although related species of the oryx are found in Africa, this is one of the few mammalian species indigenous to the Arabian peninsula. It formerly extended throughout the desert from Syria and Iraq southwards. In the Gulf region it formerly occurred in the Dahana, and at the head of the Gulf. Philby stated that it was also once abundant in the Manasir country, in the western UAE. It has certainly disappeared from this region in the wild, although one of the surviving captive herds is located in Qatar, and others are soon to be restored to the wild in Oman.

Measurements: total length 1372–1778 mm; tail 190–254 mm; ear 122 mm; greatest length of skull 248·8–312 mm.

Gazella subgutturosa   Goitred gazelle; Rhim

This is a rather heavily built gazelle, recognisable by its pale colour, with the facial, flank and gluteal stripes scarcely visible. The horns of the adult male are long and lyre-shaped, originating close together (Plate 10): females are hornless or have variably developed horns. Males have a goitre-like swelling on the throat during the breeding season.

The Rhim is the typical sand desert gazelle of Arabia, sometimes found in quite large herds and feeding on desert succulents. It does not leap or bound like other gazelles, but runs deceptively fast. It ranges from the Arabian peninsula north to south-east Asia Minor, Transcaucasia, Iran and Russian Turkestan, east to Afghanistan, and as far east as Mongolia and northern Tibet. It has been found in this region in the Kuwait area and on Bahrain Island, as well as islands west of Abu Dhabi and the western coastal regions of the UAE.

Measurements: total length 940–1194 mm; tail 131–178 mm; hind foot 232–292 mm; ear 116–127 mm; greatest length of skull 160·2–190 mm.

Gazella dorcas   Dorcas gazelle; Afri

This gazelle is not always easy to distinguish from the following species, *G. gazella,* but it is smaller and has shorter legs. The flank stripe is poorly marked, but facial stripes are usually distinct. The horns of the adult male are longer, closer together at their bases and rather straight; those of the female are also long, slender and straight.

61

The species ranges across North Africa, south to Sudan, Abyssinia and Lake Chad. It extends to the northern and western parts of the Arabian peninsula, where it is an inhabitant of the great gravel plains lying to the east of the Hejaz mountains. It is included in this book as it has been found in the vicinity of Kuwait.

Measurements: total length 928 mm; tail 90 mm; hind foot 255 mm; ear 123 mm; greatest length of skull 159·8–175·8 mm.

Gazella gazella   Mountain gazelle; Idmi
This is a larger gazelle than *G. dorcas,* with longer legs; its coloration is usually dark, with well-marked facial, flank and gluteal stripes. The adult male horns are rather short, wider apart at their bases and rather divergent from each other, the tips often strongly hooked forwards (Plate 10). Females have very short, slender horns, variably upturned at the tips.

The Mountain gazelle is found in the mountains of north-western Africa. In the Arabian peninsula, it is confined to the mountainous western, southern and eastern periphery. In the Gulf region it is confined to the Oman mountains and has been recorded from Buraimi Oasis. It is typically found in acacia country and, when disturbed, moves over broken ground with a series of spectacular and graceful bounds. It is unfortunately becoming increasingly scarce.

Measurements: total length 895–1041 mm; tail 103–108 mm; forearm 381–406 mm; hind foot 267–286 mm; ear 109·2–120 mm; greatest length of skull 164·2–196 mm.

Other species of artiodactyl that have occurred in neighbouring regions, and which might occur on the shores of the Arabian Gulf, include the Ibex (*Capra ibex*) and the Wild sheep (*Ovis ammon*), which have both been found in the mountains of Oman and are recognisable by their characteristic horns. The Wild boar (*Sus scrofa*) is found in the southern marshes of Iraq and thus could be found in the northern part of the Gulf region.

Order **LAGOMORPHA** (Lagomorphs)

The hares, rabbits and pikas comprising this order are currently regarded as quite distinct from the rodents, now included in the Rodentia. The Lagomorpha are most easily recognised by the presence of two pairs of upper incisors, of which only the front pair are functional; the minute back pair, absent in rodents, are located at their bases behind (Fig. 11). The lower cheekteeth are closer together than the upper, so that there is a lateral jaw action during chewing. A wide diastema is present as in the rodents, but there are three pairs of upper premolars and two lower ones. The large incisive foramina join together behind and the bony palate is reduced to a narrow bridge. The facial part of the maxilla is cribriform or incomplete. The fibula is joined to the calcaneum.

Only the Leporidae, which include the hares and rabbits, are represented in this region, and that by only one species of hare. They are distinguished from the little mouse-hares, or pikas, of the Ochotonidae by the elongated hind limbs and long narrow ears of the Leporidae, which also have short tufted tails and some minor differences of the skull. The hares of genus *Lepus* are widely distributed in the northern parts of the Old and New World as well as throughout the African continent. They are highly adaptable herbivores, active by day and at night, and relying on their speed to escape from predators. In association with their mode of life the young are born with the eyes open, completely furred and capable of activity.

Lepus capensis   Cape hare
The Arabian hares can hardly be confused with any other local mammals, since the elongated ears and hind feet (Plate 11), combined with two pairs of upper incisors and a

63

Fig. 11
Upper incisors of the Cape hare (*Lepus capensis*). In this view, from below and behind, the small rear pair of functionless upper incisors, present in lagomorphs but not in rodents, are seen behind the chisel-like cutting blades of the front incisors.

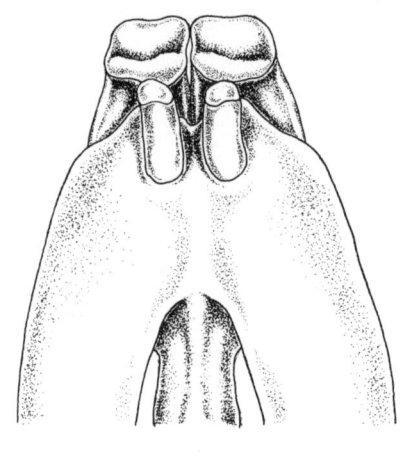

2mm

wide diastema like that of rodents, form a unique combination of characteristics.

Hares exhibit considerable local variation and even in this region several distinct sub-species occur. The tiny *L.c. omanensis* with relatively huge ears and dull greyish coat is found in the mountains of the UAE behind Sharjah. A beautiful sandy-coloured sub-species, *L.c. cheesmani,* is found in the sand deserts of Nafud, Dahana and Rub al-Khali, while a tiny hare with unusually short ears, *L.c. atallahi,* is found on Bahrain Island. The rather larger *L.c. arabicus* occurs near Kuwait.

It is one of the most versatile, mobile and adaptable of Arabian mammals, existing wherever there is sufficient vegetation to support its life. Desert hares scoop out small cave-like shelters in the sides of sandy hummocks to provide shade and concealment and their camouflage is so good that a squatting hare is seldom seen, even on open barren ground, until it is flushed.

Measurements: total length 333–502 mm; tail 30–90 mm; forearm 111·2–154 mm; hind foot 73·8–101 mm; ear 82·5–136 mm; greatest length of skull 65–87·3 mm.

Order **RODENTIA** (Rodents)

Apart from man, the rodents are without doubt the most successful group of living mammals: the 35 living families, including more than 350 genera, are of nearly world-wide distribution and have adapted to many different modes of life. Many are terrestrial, but some have become specialised for arboreal life, and a few of these are even accomplished gliders. Many species show fascinating adaptation to fossorial life, others lead an aquatic existence. Jumping forms have evolved for existence in open, barren terrain like the deserts of the Gulf region. The principal structural feature of rodents is the presence of two pairs of enlarged, ever-growing, semi-circular incisors, with chisel-like edges, separated from the cheekteeth by a wide diastema (Fig. 13). The cheekteeth are in all cases reduced in number, never exceeding twenty-eight, and in many species only twelve are present. The cheekteeth may be rooted and cease growth in the adult or retain open bases and grow persistently; their crown surface varies much in structure, sometimes high-crowned (hypsodont), sometimes low-crowned (brachyodont). The hard enamel and softer dentine and cement form patterns of cusps or folds peculiar to each group of rodents (Fig. 12). Of all living mammals this group is probably of greatest economic importance to man, and rodents are also much involved in the natural history of disease organisms.

Four families are represented in the Gulf region: the porcupines (Hystricidae) by one species; the jerboas and birch mice (Dipodidae) by two species of jerboa; the rats and mice (Muridae) by six species and the hamsters, gerbils and voles (Cricetidae) by eight species of gerbil. The seventeen species known to occur may be distinguished by

65

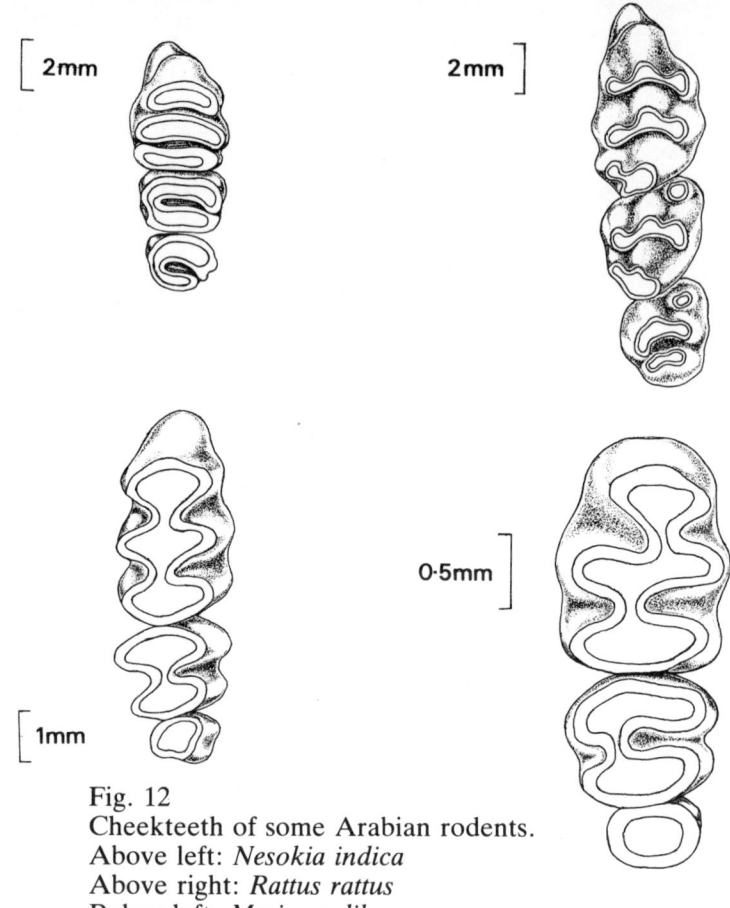

Fig. 12
Cheekteeth of some Arabian rodents.
Above left: *Nesokia indica*
Above right: *Rattus rattus*
Below left: *Meriones libycus*
Below right: *Gerbillus dasyurus*
In *Nesokia* the crown is composed of simple transverse plates, in *Rattus* the crown is cuspidate and composed essentially of three rows of cusps, in both *Meriones* and *Gerbillus* the prismatic crown of the adult is derived from two rows of cusps, which are alternated in *Gerbillus,* but form simple transverse prisms in *Meriones*.
The right upper cheekteeth of each are shown, reproduced by stereomicroscopic drawings at differing magnifications.

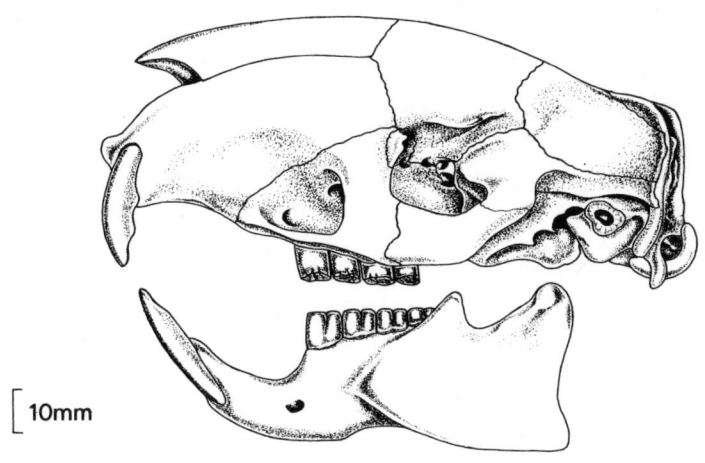

10mm

Fig. 13
Skull of the Indian crested porcupine (*Hystrix indica*). The Crested porcupine, a member of the Hystricidae, is the largest Arabian rodent. The enlarged single pair of chisel-like upper incisors and large diastema are typical of rodents. The nasal bones and cavity of the porcupine are greatly enlarged and four upper and lower cheekteeth are present.

the key given below and one other species that may occur is briefly mentioned in the text.

Key to the Rodentia (Rodents) of the Arabian Gulf

Very large rodent (total length more than 750 mm)
Body and tail protected by long rigid spines
   . . . Porcupines (Hystricidae)
      . . . *Hystrix indica*

Small or medium-sized rodents, not exceeding 500 mm in total length.

Coat furry, or if spinous then mouse-sized (see *Acomys* below)

Hind feet grossly enlarged (51–65·7 mm)
  . . . Jerboas (Dipodidae)

> Five toes present, two of which are vestigial, the three functional toes lacking prominent tufts of hair (Fig. 14)
>   . . . *Allactaga euphratica*

> Only three toes present, with prominent tufts of hair (Fig. 14)
>   . . . *Jaculus jaculus*

Hind feet not grossly enlarged, not exceeding 45 mm:

Tympanic bullae not grossly enlarged, their greatest diameter from front to back less than or at most subequal with the greatest width across the two rows of upper cheekteeth
  . . . Rats and mice (Muridae)

> Fur of back spiny:
>   Soles of feet black
>   Spiny covering extends forward to occipital region
>   . . . *Acomys russatus*

>   Soles of feet pale
>   Spiny covering limited to lower back
>   . . . *Acomys dimidiatus*

> Coat furry:
>   Rat-sized rodents (adults more than 240 mm in total length):
>   Crowns of cheekteeth composed of simple transverse plates, no cusps present
>   . . . *Nesokia indica*

>   Crowns of cheekteeth cuspidate:
>   Tail distinctly shorter than head and body
>   . . . *Rattus norvegicus*
>   Tail longer than the head and body
>   . . . *Rattus rattus*

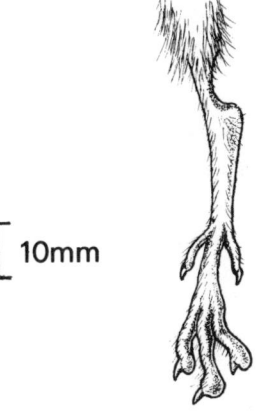 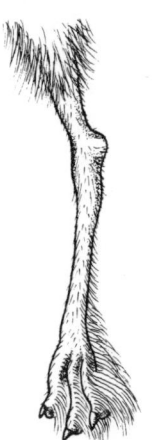

10mm

Fig. 14
Foot of Euphrates jerboa (*Allactaga euphratica*) on left, and Lesser jerboa (*Jaculus jaculus*) on right. Left foot of each, natural size. In *Allactaga* five toes are present, three of which are functional, in *Jaculus* only three toes remain, which are furnished with tufts of stiff hair.

> Mouse-sized rodents (total length less than 177 mm)
> . . . *Mus musculus*

Tympanic bullae grossly enlarged, their greatest diameter from front to back clearly exceeding the greatest width across the two rows of upper cheekteeth
> . . . Gerbils (Cricetidae)

> Tail bushy throughout almost entire length, usually with contrasting white and grey tuft at the end
> . . . *Sekeetamys calurus*

> Tail only tufted at the end, not so coloured:
>> Heavily-built, rat-like gerbils; tail with at least a small black tuft at the end:
>> Tail black throughout its length above and below Sides contrastingly pale
>> . . . *Tatera indica*

Tail with black tuft at the end only:
Claws of hind feet white
. . . *Meriones crassus*
Claws of hind feet black:
Tail usually longer than head and body
Black tail tip well developed
. . . *Meriones libycus*
Tail clearly shorter than head and body
Black tail tip much reduced
. . . *Psammomys obesus*
Lightly built, mouse-like gerbils, tail tuft greyish
or pallid, never with defined black tip:
Soles of feet hairy
. . . *Gerbillus cheesmani*
Soles of feet naked
Tympanic bullae smaller, mastoid portions do
not project beyond occiput
. . . *Gerbillus dasyurus*
Tympanic bullae larger, mastoid portions project
beyond occiput
. . . *Gerbillus nanus*

Fam. **Hystricidae** (Porcupines)

Hystrix indica   Indian crested porcupine
This is the largest Arabian rodent, and its protective covering of rigid creamy-white and brown-banded quills is quite
characteristic (Plate 11). The short tail is armed with a
cluster of specialised 'rattling quills'; the end of each of
these is widened and hollow. The coarse coat forms a
pronounced mane down the back and is blackish brown in
colour, but on the sides of the neck the creamy white tips of
the bristles produce a semicircular white collar. The skull is
remarkable for the enlarged nasal bones and greatly inflated nasal cavity (Fig. 13).

The Indian crested porcupine is probably more widely
distributed in the Arabian peninsula than the few scattered

records suggest; in the Gulf region it was noted by H. R. P. Dickson as common in the Summan area near Safa in Saudi Arabia. It is a nocturnal animal, living in large burrows. It is colonial, the colonies sometimes covering quite a large area. Caves, rock crevices and ruined human dwellings are often inhabited. Damage to crops by porcupines may be considerable – turnip is especially favoured. The porcupine is itself regarded as a delicacy by the Beduin. When attacked, the porcupine charges backwards, inflicting severe wounds with its spines, which sometimes become detached in the attacker's flesh.

Measurements: total length 790–985 mm; tail 105–175 mm; hind foot 87–100 mm; ear 40–44 mm; greatest length of skull 134·9–148·7 mm.

Fam. **Dipodidae** (Jerboas, birch mice)

Allactaga euphratica　　　　　　　　　　　　Euphrates jerboa
This elegant jerboa is at once recognisable by the presence of five toes on the greatly enlarged hind feet (Fig. 14), unlike the common *Jaculus*, which has only three. Only the three central toes are functional, however, the outer ones being vestigial and situated high up the foot. The tip of the tail is furnished with a beautiful tricoloured white, black and white brush, which serves as a signal 'flag' when the animal bounds about. The ears are very tall and narrow, the forelimbs short and puny, and the whiskers well developed (Plate 12).

Allactaga euphratica is a steppe jerboa confined to the northern parts of the Arabian peninsula and in the Gulf region known only in the vicinity of Kuwait. It is strictly nocturnal and lives in burrows; it will forage at least 0·25 km away from the burrow at night, relying on its amazing agility and speed to escape from predators with acrobatic leaps and bounds. This species always seems rarer than the Lesser jerboa where the two species occur together.

Measurements: total length 230–310 mm; tail 144–195 mm; hind foot 50–61 mm; ear 27–42 mm.

Jaculus jaculus   Lesser jerboa
This is the common jerboa of Arabia, readily distinguishable from the preceding species by the presence of
only three toes on the hind foot, which further differ in
having prominent tufts of stiff hair (Fig. 14). A prominent
black and white 'flag' is present on the tail tip, but the ears
are shorter than *Allactaga,* the eyes large and lustrous and
the whiskers particularly well developed (Plate 12).

This species is found throughout the entire Arabian
peninsula wherever a suitable sand desert habitat exists,
and it is known from the whole Arabian Gulf shore as well
as Bahrain Island. It is probably one of the mammals best
adapted to desert conditions, constructing its burrows in
sandy areas and foraging far afield. The presence of skulls
of this species in the pellets of birds of prey shows that its
remarkable powers of evasion do not always protect it from
predatory birds. In periods of intense heat, jerboas probably aestivate, subsisting on stores of dried seeds in their
sealed burrows in a condition of reduced activity. In captivity they do not drink and appear to derive all the moisture they need from their vegetable food.

Measurements: total length 246–317 mm; tail 128–203
mm; hind foot 51–64 mm; greatest length of skull 30·5–
35·2 mm.

Fam. **Muridae** (Rats, mice)

Acomys russatus   Golden spiny mouse
The spiny mice are immediately recognisable by a spiny
protection over the lower part of the back. In *A. russatus*
the spines extend further forward than in *A. dimidiatus*,
reaching the back of the head and, in addition, the palms
and soles are black (Fig. 15). The tail of *A. russatus* is
always considerably shorter than the head and body and
the golden-brown coloration of the back is also characteristic.

The Golden spiny mouse occurs mainly in the rocky
western parts of the peninsula. It is included in this book

because Dr W. Büttiker recently found it in Wadi Khumra, in eastern Saudi Arabia. This species is found in rocky habitats, but unlike *A. dimidiatus* it is diurnal and may be seen darting about from one rock crevice to another during the midday heat. It is believed that the blackish coloration of the skin confers some protection from the effects of solar radiation. The Golden spiny mouse is certainly very well adapted to life in arid and hot conditions, with remarkable temperature regulation and kidney function.

Measurements: total length 115–190 mm; tail 57–75 mm; hind foot 15–19·5 mm; ear 13–19 mm; greatest length of skull 25·9–30·4 mm.

Acomys dimidiatus   Spiny mouse

This is the common Arabian spiny mouse, distinguishable from the preceding species by the limitation of the spiny armature to the lower back and also by the pale, flesh-coloured soles and palms. When complete, the tail is always relatively longer than that of *A. russatus*, being as long as the head and body combined or even longer (Fig. 15).

A. dimidiatus ranges more widely in the Arabian peninsula, occurring almost wherever suitable rocky habitats exist. In this region it occurs in eastern Saudi Arabia and it is known from the mountains of the UAE, where M. D. Gallagher found it at Jebel Faiyah. This spiny mouse favours a similar rocky habitat to that selected by the Golden spiny mouse, but its activity is predominantly nocturnal and crepuscular. The Spiny mouse moves about with lightning speed in rock crevices, where its presence can often be detected by its droppings and the scattered debris of its diet of seeds of desert plants.

Measurements: total length 158–247 mm; tail 75–138 mm; hind foot 16·2–21 mm; ear 15–24 mm; greatest length of skull 27·2–33·4 mm.

Nesokia indica   Short-tailed bandicoot rat

A medium-sized, rat-like rodent with short, scaly tail and

[10mm

Fig. 15
Left: Spiny mouse (*Acomys dimidiatus*)
Right: Golden spiny mouse (*Acomys russatus*).
In *Acomys russatus* the ears are smaller, the tail shorter and the spines begin on the crown of the head, unlike *A. dimidiatus* in which the spines only extend to the middle of the back. In *A. russatus* the soles of the feet are black.

brown fur, this species superficially resembles *Rattus norvegicus*. It is, however, readily distinguished from the latter by the cheekteeth, which are composed of simple transverse plates without trace of cusps in adults (Fig. 12). The skull is short and broad, unlike the long, narrow cranium of the Brown rat.

N. indica is found mainly in the northern parts of the Arabian peninsula, extending southwards along the Arabian Gulf littoral of Saudi Arabia, where it is known from 'Uqair and Sayhat. It is a colonial rodent forming extensive burrow systems with characteristic earth diggings at the burrow entrances along the banks of irrigation channels. It is often found associated with camel thorn scrub and is rather difficult to trap. If the earth plug at the entrance to its burrow is removed, the bandicoot will emerge to replace it, but this fossorial rodent seldom ventures far from the burrow system unless flooded out.

Measurements: total length 240–370 mm; tail 97–131 mm; hind foot 31–39 mm; ear 16–22 mm; greatest length of skull 36·3–46·9 mm.

Rattus norvegicus   Brown rat; Norway rat

This rat is distinguishable from *R. rattus* by its heavier build, the tail being always shorter than the head and body. The skull has a narrower braincase and the front upper molar lacks an outer-front cusp. The coloration is dull ochre/buff above, the belly being white with greyish hair bases.

The Brown rat is an immigrant species found in the vicinity of seaports throughout Arabia. In the Gulf region it has been found on Bahrain Island and recently, by Dr W. Büttiker, in eastern Saudi Arabia at Dammam and Hofuf. It is a bold and destructive rodent, active both by day and by night. It is a less active climber than *R. rattus* and is often found in warehouses, cellars, sewers, slaughterhouses and garbage tips. It is a carrier of human diseases, such as plague and Weil's disease.

Measurements: total length 312–490 mm; tail 118–220

mm; hind foot 35–45 mm; ear 19–25 mm; greatest length of skull 40·4–51·2 mm.

Rattus rattus   House rat; Black rat
This species is readily distinguishable from the preceding by its slender build and longer tail, which is almost always longer than the head and body. The ear is somewhat larger but the skull is smaller with the braincase relatively broad, and the first upper molar has a distinct outer-front cusp. Coloration is very variable, and polymorphic, melanistic rats are not often seen in the Gulf region, where the back is usually brown or grey-brown and the belly white or pale yellow.

The Black rat is also an immigrant rodent, limited to the vicinity of seaports and with only limited spread into the interior in Arabia. In the Gulf region it has been found on Bahrain and in a number of localities in eastern Saudi Arabia. It is a more versatile and adaptable rat than *R. norvegicus* and is an agile climber, often inhabiting roofs and upper storeys of buildings. It is of great significance in public health and has been the source of many terrible pandemics of plague throughout history, passing on the disease by means of the rat flea *Xenopsylla cheopis*.

Measurements: total length 238–400 mm; tail 104–240 mm; hind foot 27–38 mm; ear 17·2–29 mm; greatest length of skull 34·4–43·9 mm.

Mus musculus   House mouse
The House mouse is one of the smallest Arabian rodents. It is readily distinguished from the other murids of the Gulf region by its teeth, and particularly by the presence of a distinct notch behind the cutting edge of the upper incisor (Fig. 16); the first upper molar is enlarged, equal to the second and third combined, and the first row of its cusps is distorted, the inner cusp in line with the middle cusp of the second row. The eyes are small and the hind foot short, the back usually clay-coloured and the belly white, but much variation occurs.

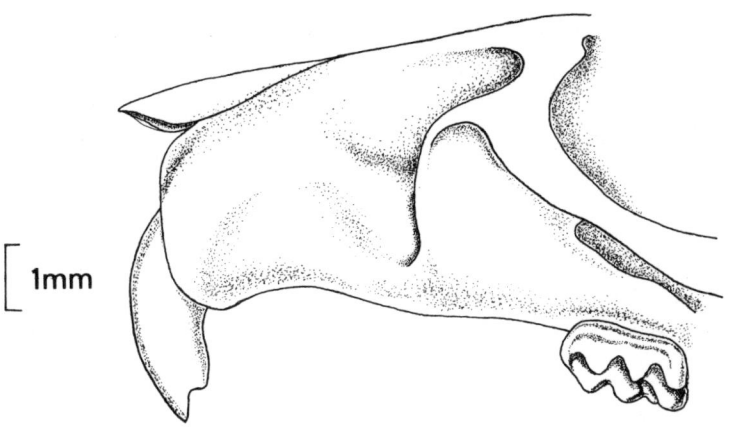

1mm

Fig. 16
Upper incisor tooth of the House mouse (*Mus musculus*). In the House mouse there is usually a well-marked notch in the upper incisor just below the cutting edge when viewed from the side.

This adaptable little rodent, widespread in Arabia, is known from most parts of the Gulf region. Although often commensal with man, and thus common in gardens and towns, it also occurs as a wild, feral form in Arabia and it has been found inhabiting the same burrows as such strict desert rodents as *Meriones crassus*. It is evident, however, that, like the rats, the House mouse has not penetrated far inland from the coastal regions in Arabia and it has not been found in the central deserts. A very tiny sub-species, *M.m. gentilulus* occurs on Bahrain and in the UAE, while the larger *M.m. praetextus* is found from Hofuf northwards.

Measurements: total length 111–177 mm; tail 54–94 mm; hind foot 14·5–20 mm; ear 9–15 mm; greatest length of skull 17·6–23·8 mm.

Fam. **Cricetidae** (Hamsters, gerbils, voles)

Sekeetamys calurus   Bushy-tailed jird

This elegant gerbil is the size of a large mouse and can be recognised by its long tail, which is bushy for more than half its length and usually ends in a handsome grey and white tuft resembling the flag of the jerboa (Fig. 17). The soles of the hind feet are naked and the tympanic bullae of the skull are large, projecting beyond the occiput. The long, soft fur is sandy-brown above and white on the belly, the eyes and ears are well developed and the whiskers long.

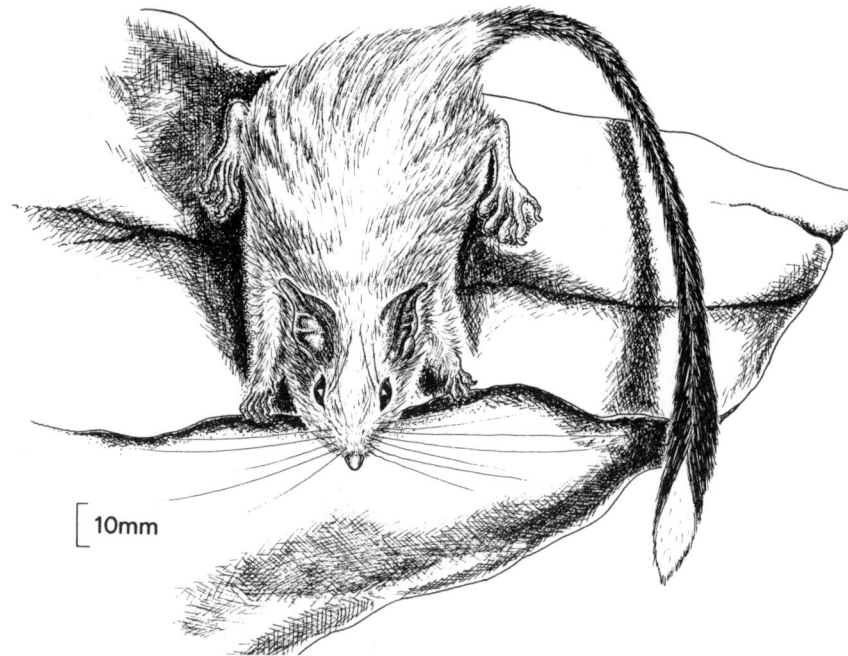

10mm

Fig. 17
Bushy-tailed jird (*Sekeetamys calurus*). *Sekeetamys* is readily recognisable amongst Arabian gerbils by its heavily furred tail, the tuft on the end of which is black, usually with a contrasting white tip.

Originally considered to be confined to Sinai, the Eastern Egyptian Desert and Jordan, *S. calurus* has recently been found in Saudi Arabia. Dr Iyad Nader first found it in the Tuwayq Mountains and, more recently, Dr W. Büttiker obtained a specimen at Jebel Banban – hence its inclusion here. It is nocturnal and specially adapted for life in the arid mountain ranges of the peninsula, climbing with great agility amongst the boulders and granite fragments which litter the precipitous slopes, and beneath which it constructs its burrows. The burrow entrances are often littered with the seeds and remnants of vegetation that form its diet.

Measurements: total length 234–274 mm; tail 112–148 mm; hind foot 29·3–33 mm; ear 17–19 mm; greatest length of skull 33·5–37·5 mm.

Tatera indica   Indian gerbil; Antelope rat

This robust, rat-like gerbil is easily mistaken for an ordinary rat until the peculiar coloration of the long tail is appreciated. The tail is fully haired with a black tuft at the end and, uniquely, is coloured black above and below with sharply contrasting pale sides (apart from the terminal tuft) throughout its length. The upper surface of the head and body is tawny greyish, the belly white; the ears are rather large and the soles naked. The zygomatic plate of the skull projects further forward than in Sand rats (*Meriones*).

T. indica is an Indo-Asiatic gerbil ranging from the Indian peninsula westwards through Iran to the river plains of Iraq and Syria. In the Gulf region, it is only known from the vicinity of Kuwait. It is an inhabitant of agricultural country, not usually found in very arid terrain and seems more water-dependent than most gerbils. A colonial animal, it constructs large warrens and at times causes considerable damage to crops. It plays an important part in the natural history of plague in the Middle East. Possessing a high degree of resistance itself, it forms a reservoir of infection and, having a tendency to enter human habitations and farm settlements, it has many opportunities to transmit the disease to other commensal rodents and hence to man.

Measurements: total length 330–430 mm; tail 167–220 mm; hind foot 40–45 mm; ear 25–29 mm; greatest length of skull 43·9–49·2 mm.

Meriones crassus — Sundevall's jird

This is one of the commonest desert rodents in Arabia. It is recognisable by the presence of a distinct black tuft at the end of the tail, although the tuft is less well developed than in the following species, *M. libycus.* Unlike that species, the claws are pale. The tympanic bullae are enormously inflated and the suprameatal triangle is open at the back. The hair of the back is sandy buff, with distinct white tufts behind the ears, and the belly is white. The soles are hairy except for naked patches under the heels.

M. crassus occurs throughout the greater part of the Arabian peninsula, mainly in sandy desert terrain. It is known from numerous localities throughout most of the Arabian Gulf shore and was recently found on Howar Island. It is a colonial gerbil, constructing warrens in sandy hummocks in the desert, often situated beneath the roots of thorny bushes. Unlike *M. libycus,* this species is mainly crepuscular and nocturnal.

Measurements: total length 219–290 mm; tail 107–150 mm; hind foot 25–35 mm; ear 14–19 mm; greatest length of skull 32·5–42·6 mm.

Meriones libycus — Libyan jird

This is a more robust jird than the preceding species, from which it is readily distinguished by the more extensive black tuft at the end of the tail and by the black claws; the skin of the ears is also blackish inside. The tympanic bullae are not quite as inflated as in *M. crassus* and the suprameatal triangle is closed at the back. The long tail, with more extensive black tuft, and grooved upper incisors help to distinguish this handsome jird from *Psammomys obesus* (see below).

80

The Libyan jird extends across North Africa and the northern parts of the Arabian peninsula east to Iran, Transcaucasia, Russian and Chinese Turkestan and Afghanistan. It occurs throughout the Gulf region, where the reddish sandy sub-species *M.l. syrius* is found as far south as Hofuf, while the pale *M.l. arimalius* was described from Jabrin and has also been found in the UAE near Buraimi. It is also a colonial jird, found in similar situations to *M. crassus,* but its activity tends to be more diurnal. It often holds the black tufted tail erect when running from one burrow to another. It will consume even the bitter gourds of the donkey melon (*Citrullus colocynthis*). R. E. Cheesman noted the curious ticking noises emitted by *M.l. arimalius* when hiding in its burrow from suspected danger.

Measurements: total length 255–344 mm; tail 117–190 mm; hind foot 33–41 mm; ear 16–22 mm; greatest length of skull 35–45·5 mm.

Psammomys obesus   Fat jird

This jird superficially resembles *Meriones libycus* since it also has black claws, blackish skin inside the ear and is much the same size. However, its tail is much shorter and has a greatly reduced black tuft at the tip (Fig. 18). The ungrooved upper incisors of the Fat jird distinguish it from all other Arabian gerbils. The ears are small, while the coloration is a pale sandy colour above and white on the belly.

The species ranges across North Africa, extending to the northern deserts and steppes of Arabia. In the Gulf region it is only known from eastern Saudi Arabia. This is a colonial jird which constructs large warrens; its apparently local occurrence seems due to its dependence on succulent desert plants from the foliage of which it obtains moisture. It is thus a rather specialised desert rodent, but at times is destructive to crops such as barley.

Measurements: total length 205–435 mm; tail 95–152 mm; hind foot 30–42 mm; ear 13·5–18 mm; greatest length of skull 36·3–48 mm.

20mm

Fig. 18
Fat jird (*Psammomys obesus*). This rat-sized gerbil has a short tail with a poorly developed black tuft, black claws and small ears.

Gerbillus cheesmani   Cheesman's gerbil
This elegant little gerbil is readily recognised amongst the small, mouse-like gerbils of the region by the beautiful, pale sandy-buff coloration of its back and the hairy soles of its feet (Fig. 19). The tympanic bullae of the skull are greatly inflated, projecting just beyond the occiput. The undersurface, feet and tail are white, the tuft of the tail-tip greyish-white. There are prominent white spots above the lustrous black eyes and behind the ears. The whiskers are long.

Cheesman's gerbil ranges from Iraq southwards throughout the Arabian peninsula and is probably also represented in Iran. It is known throughout the Gulf region where it is represented by the very pale and long-tailed sub-species, *G.c. arduus*. It is a strictly nocturnal gerbil and, as it favours a true sand desert habitat, is designated a

10mm

Fig. 19
Cheesman's gerbil (*Gerbillus cheesmani*). This elegant, pale gerbil is a sand desert species. The soles of the feet are hairy and the toes fringed with white hairs.

83

'psammophilic' gerbil. The colouring is extremely well adapted to the desert habitat. Unlike many gerbils it is not colonial, living in a small hole with a single entrance; only small numbers are usually found in a particular area.

Measurements: total length 170–235 mm; tail 94–135 mm; hind foot 24–33 mm; ear 9–15 mm; greatest length of skull 26·1–31 mm.

Gerbillus nanus   Baluchistan gerbil
This and the following species, *G. dasyurus,* can be distinguished from *G. cheesmani* by their naked soles, duller fawn-brown coloration on their backs and darker, greyish tail tufts. They are scarcely distinguishable from each other externally, but the skulls are quite distinctive: in this species the tympanic bullae are much inflated, projecting behind the occiput and the upper part of the eardrum (tympanic membrane) is not formed of bone.

G. nanus ranges from Baluchistan through southern Iran and the whole southern part of the Arabian peninsula to north and north-east Africa. In the Gulf region, it is known near Kuwait, in eastern Saudi Arabia and in the UAE. It is a crepuscular and nocturnal gerbil, forming colonies in saline flats and semi-desert terrain. In some parts of Arabia, local substrate races have evolved by natural selection to resemble very closely the soil colour of their habitats. It is sometimes found sharing the burrow systems of other gerbils, like *Meriones,* and will wander far afield at night to forage, employing well-established trails and making use of all available concealment from the sharp eyes of owls and other predators.

Measurements: total length 165–235 mm; tail 80–145 mm; hind foot 20–28 mm; ear 7–14·5 mm; greatest length of skull 24·3–29·6 mm.

Gerbillus dasyurus   Wagner's gerbil
Wagner's gerbil (Fig. 20) is difficult to distinguish from *G. nanus* by its external features, but the skull is immediately recognisable by its smaller tympanic bullae, which do not

Fig. 20
Wagner's gerbil (*Gerbillus dasyurus*). This little
gerbil, which lives in rocky steppe, has the soles of
the feet naked, the toes without hairy fringes and
the tail tufted with grey.

project beyond the occiput, while the upper part of the
eardrum (tympanic membrane) is formed of bone.

This species is indigenous to the Arabian peninsula,
where it is widely distributed. *G.d. dasyurus* is known from
the Hasa in eastern Saudi Arabia, while a very dark sub-
species, *G.d. gallagheri,* with a blackish tail and dusky
soles to the feet, is found in the mountains of the UAE,
near Masafi. *G. dasyurus* favours a quite different terrain
from *G. nanus,* being almost always found in rocky places;
thus in Saudi Arabia it tends to occur in the same limestone
escarpments and boulder slopes as *Sekeetamys calurus,*
and Dr W. Büttiker did indeed trap both species at Jebel
Banban. Its food mainly consists of the seeds of annual
herbs like *Medicago* and its burrows are often located
beneath loose slabs of rock. Like *G. nanus,* it is strictly
nocturnal, but it is not colonial. It also has been found
co-existing with *Meriones* species.

Measurements: total length 149–227 mm; tail 81–131 mm; hind foot 20–26·5 mm; ear 10–15·5 mm; greatest length of the skull 23·2–29·3 mm.

Another species of gerbil, *Gerbillus mesopotamiae,* occurs in the plains of Iraq along the Tigris and Euphrates Rivers and may perhaps occur in the northern part of the Gulf region. It is distinguishable from *G. nanus* and *G. dasyurus* by its untufted tail, darker coloration of the back, and blackish cheek patches, but certain identification depends on detailed examination of the tympanic bullae, which are small like those of *G. dasyurus,* but with the tympanic membrane not formed of bone like that of *G. nanus.*

References

Corbett, G. B. (1978): *The Mammals of the Palaearctic Region: a taxonomic review.* London: British Museum (Natural History) pp. 314.
(This is the most recent checklist and taxonomic review of the mammals of the whole Palaearctic region.)

Harrison, D. L. (1964): *The Mammals of Arabia; Vol. 1. Insectivora. Chiroptera. Primates.* London: Benn pp. 1–192.
Harrison, D. L. (1968): *The Mammals of Arabia; Vol. 2. Carnivora. Hyracoidea. Artiodactyla.* London: Benn pp. 193–381.
Harrison, D. L. (1972): *The Mammals of Arabia; Vol. 3. Lagomorpha. Rodentia.* London: Benn pp. 382–670.
(This is a comprehensive treatment of the terrestrial mammals of the whole Arabian peninsula, with a full Bibliography relevant to the region up to the time of publication. These works are intended for readers with specialist knowledge.)

87

Index

Principal references to the species listed below are denoted in bold type

89

91

92